Cambridge IGCSE® and O Level

Business Studies

Revision Guide

Revised second edition

Medi Houghton

CAMBRIDGE
UNIVERSITY PRESS

CAMBRIDGE
UNIVERSITY PRESS

Shaftesbury Road, Cambridge CB2 8EA, United Kingdom

One Liberty Plaza, 20th Floor, New York, NY 10006, USA

477 Williamstown Road, Port Melbourne, VIC 3207, Australia

314–321, 3rd Floor, Plot 3, Splendor Forum, Jasola District Centre, New Delhi – 110025, India

103 Penang Road, #05-06/07, Visioncrest Commercial, Singapore 238467

Cambridge University Press is part of the University of Cambridge.

It furthers the University's mission by disseminating knowledge in the pursuit of education, learning and research at the highest international levels of excellence.

www.cambridge.org
Information on this title: www.cambridge.org/9781108441742

© Cambridge University Press & Assessment 2018

First published 2013
Second edition 2016
Revised second edition 2018

20 19 18 17 16 15 14 13 12 11 10

Printed in Great Britain by Ashford Colour Press Ltd.

A catalogue record for this publication is available from the British Library

ISBN 978-1-108-44174-2 Paperback

Cover image: Frederic Cirou/Getty Images

Table of contents

How to use this book

Learning summary – A summary list of key topics and concepts that you will be looking at in this chapter, to help with navigation through the book and give a reminder of what's important about each topic for your revision.

Worked example

For Z Foods in 2016, gross profit was $90m, revenue was $150m.

To calculate the gross profit margin:

$$\frac{90}{150} \times 100 = \textbf{60 \%}$$

What does this mean? It shows the business made 60 cents in gross profit for every dollar of revenue in 2016.

Is this good? You would need to compare the result with 2015 to see if this has improved or not:

2015 data:

Gross profit margin = $60/120 \times 100 = 50\%$

2016 vs 2015: the ratio has improved indicating the margin has increased.

Sample question

Jian owns a restaurant in the city centre. His menu changes daily, depending on what meat and vegetables are available. All ingredients are bought locally which helps to keep costs low. Jian is always trying to increase added value.

Explain **two** ways that Jian could increase added value. **[6]**

Sample answer:
Way 1: Jian can buy in the meat and vegetables at low cost and turn them into finished dishes for the customers, so there is a greater difference between the cost to make the dishes and price charged for them. **[3]**

Way 2: Provide a good customer service to customers in the restaurant. This adds to the experience, so customers are willing to pay more for a meal rather than go to cheaper places. **[3]**

Worked example - Guidance on how to answer a particular question, emphasising the different stages you will need to work through to get to your answer.

Sample question and answer – an example of a question with a suggested answer.

TIP

Always look at the context. Suitable options will vary with the type of product. Use the context to improve your answer. Remember: for application, you must link the point to the scenario.

Tip – quick suggestions to remind you about key facts and highlight important points.

Summary

This unit covers a number of basic ideas. The fact that resources are limited means that businesses have to decide how best to use the factors of production. Specialisation can help. A business will try to add value at every stage of production as this can help make a profit.

Summary – A summary of what you have learned within the chapter.

TERMS

Opportunity cost: the cost of something in terms of the next best option.

Scarcity: limited availability of resources to meet the unlimited wants of people.

Progress check

1 Define 'scarcity'.

2 What is the difference between a need and a want? Give an example of each.

3 Explain what is the main purpose of business activity.

4 State **two** factors of production for a market trader.

Progress check – check your own knowledge and see how well you are getting on by answering regular questions.

Terms – clear and straightforward explanations are provided for the most important words in each topic. Key terms appear in bold within the main text.

Examination-style questions

Question 1

Ravel is a farmer in country A. He has been looking at some data, shown in Table 2.02. He cannot understand why there is a difference in employment between countries. Both countries have a mixed economy.

	Country A	**Country B**
Primary sector	45	10
Secondary sector	20	20
Tertiary	35	70

Table 2.02 Percentage of labour force employed in each country.

NOTE: Population of each country is 60 million.

a Identify **one** type of business that could be found in the:

primary sector

secondary sector. [2]

b Calculate the number of people employed in the tertiary sector in country A. [2]

c Explain **two** possible reasons for the difference in the percentage of labour employed in different sectors in each country. [8]

Question 2

SRT makes a wide range of paints. These are sold to businesses and customers in many countries. Market research is important. The Managing Director said, 'Different countries have different legal standards for paint. Customers want different colours and sizes of tins.' SRT uses the services of many businesses from the tertiary sector.

Explain **four** important tertiary sector businesses that SRT might use. [8]

Examination-style questions – Exam-style questions for you to test your knowledge and understanding at the end of each chapter. The answers are provided at the back of the book.

Introduction

This revision guide has been written to help students studying for Cambridge IGCSE or O Level Business Studies.

Each chapter includes:

- definitions and explanations of key concepts
- summary charts or diagrams to highlight important ideas
- tips and notes to provide helpful guidance on key points
- progress checks to allow you to test your understanding
- sample questions and answers to highlight common mistakes or misunderstandings
- sample examination-style questions for you to practise.

Assessment objectives (AOs)

Business Studies is a skills-based subject so remember to show evidence of the skills below as well as knowledge.

1 **Knowledge** – showing your knowledge and understanding of terms, concepts, theories and techniques.

- Be precise with any definitions.
- Learn the main facts and issues.

2 **Application** – using knowledge and understanding of terms, concepts, theories and techniques for a variety of business problems or issues.

- Avoid making general statements.
- Not all points may be relevant, so focus your answer on the given scenario.

3 **Analysis** – selecting, explaining or interpreting information to show good understanding of terms and effects of decision.

- Do not just list points.
- Try to develop your answer to show the consequences of what the points might mean for the business.

4 **Evaluation** – presenting developed arguments or reasoned explanations, and being able to make judgements and decisions.

- Make a decision, and explain how or why you hold this view.
- Focus on developing relevant points (for and/or against) to support what YOU are saying. Remember: a decision on its own is not enough.

Command words

Use any command words given as a guide to help you answer the question. Each will tell you which skills are required for each question.

Use the marks as a guide to how much you should write. More marks available for a question means that a wider range of skills are likely to be needed.

Let's look at a sample answer to highlight how each skill could be shown:

knowledge

Sample question

KOKO has ten seafood restaurants in the city. The Human Resources manager is looking to recruit a new manager for one restaurant. He cannot decide whether to use internal or external recruitment.

Do you think KOKO should use internal or external recruitment? Justify your answer. **[6]**

analysis

Sample answer

With internal recruitment the owners will know what the person is like so will know that the person has the relevant experience and is suitable for the job. If the person has worked for them in the kitchen for several years, it will be clear whether they will be able to do the job of restaurant manager. Recruiting someone from outside could be a risk. They might have new ideas but these might not be appropriate for this type of restaurant, so damaging its reputation. So I think it is better to use internal recruitment to ensure the standards are maintained.

evaluation   application

Preparing for examination

1 **Know what you need to learn.** Ask your teacher for a copy of the syllabus. This outlines all the content you need to focus on when you revise.

2 **Make a revision timetable.** Set aside time every week for study. If you have examinations in more than one subject, allow time to revise for everything.

3 **Revise effectively.** Split up your time into smaller revision periods, say 30 to 40 minutes. Breaks can give you time to reflect on what you have learnt.

4 **Make your revision active.** Make notes, summary charts, mnemonics, think of picture associations for key themes so you can remember ideas later.

5 **Check yourself regularly to check that you have understood.**

6 **Practise past or sample questions** so you are familiar with examination-style questions. It will also help you to practise writing answers in a particular timeframe.

Remember to:

1 **Read each question carefully.** Look for the command words.

2 Always **show your workings for calculations**.

3 **Develop points** to show how or why they might matter.

4 Try to **base your answers on the scenario** given.

5 If a question **asks for a decision, make one, and support it.**

Section 1:
UNDERSTANDING
BUSINESS ACTIVITY

Business activity

1.01 Needs and wants

Needs are things that we must have to survive such as shelter, clothing and food. Wants are things that we would like to have to make our lives more enjoyable.

People can live without satisfying their wants, but not without meeting their needs.

1.02 Scarcity and opportunity cost

Scarcity of resources creates a basic economic problem. Resources are limited but people's wants are not. Choices must be made. Resources used to make one thing cannot be used for another purpose. The value of the option not selected is known as the opportunity cost.

Worked example

Business A is a retailer. Next to the shop the business owns a large plot of land. The business can either use the space to extend the shop or turn it into a customer car park. It decides to extend the shop. The opportunity cost is the car park.

TERMS

Opportunity cost: the cost of something in terms of the next best option.

Scarcity: limited availability of resources to meet the unlimited wants of people.

1.03 Importance of specialisation

Most production involves more than one person or piece of equipment. People and businesses specialise, to try not to waste limited resources. This can involve division of labour where employees are given a specific job to do. This should lead to:

- less wastage of scarce resources

- lower production costs

- greater output from same amount of resources.

TERM

Specialisation: when people and businesses focus on activities they are best at.

1.04 The purpose of business activity

All businesses use factors of production to make goods or provide services, in order to satisfy people's needs and wants.

These factors of production can be classified into four main groups:

Type of factor	Description of factor
Land	includes all natural resources as well as the space used for production
Labour	the employees
Capital	the finance, machinery and buildings used to produce goods and services
Enterprise	the people who organise the land, labour and capital

Table 1.01 The four factors of production.

> **TIP**
> Capital has many meanings in business. Make sure you understand what it refers to in a given situation.

> **TIP**
> A business can be one person, a large global company employing thousands of people or even a charity.

1.05 Adding value

Most businesses buy resources to make products. These raw materials are altered to make them worth more money, so the business can sell them at a higher price.

Worked example

Tickers make watches. The materials cost $50 and Tickers sell the finished watches for $150. Tickers pay employees $60. Other costs including rent are $15. What is the added value? The answer is: $100.

This is not all profit. Only the amount left after all the costs have been covered is profit: $25.

> **TIP**
> Remember that added value is NOT the same as profit.

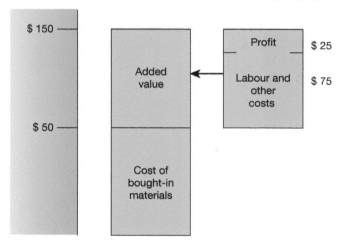

Figure 1.01 Summary chart: added value at Tickers.

Ways for a business to increase added value include:

- make raw materials into finished goods
- branding
- packaging
- add extra features to products
- improve customer service.

> **TERM**
> Added value: the difference between the selling price of a product and the cost of raw materials used to make it.

Sample question

Jian owns a restaurant in the city centre. His menu changes daily, depending on what meat and vegetables are available. All ingredients are bought locally which helps to keep costs low. Jian is always trying to increase added value.

Explain **two** ways that Jian could increase added value. [6]

Sample answer:
Way 1: Jian can buy in the meat and vegetables at low cost and turn them into finished dishes for the customers, so there is a greater difference between the cost to make the dishes and price charged for them. [3]

Way 2: Provide a good customer service to customers in the restaurant. This adds to the experience, so customers are willing to pay more for a meal rather than go to cheaper places. [3]

> **TIP**
> Always look at the context. Suitable options will vary with the type of product. Use the context to improve your answer. Remember: for application, you must link the point to the scenario.

> **TIP**
> Simply using the name of the business is not classed as application.

Summary

This unit covers a number of basic ideas. The fact that resources are limited means that businesses have to decide how best to use the factors of production. Specialisation can help. A business will try to add value at every stage of production as this can help make a profit.

Progress check

1 Define 'scarcity'.

2 What is the difference between a need and a want? Give an example of each.

3 Explain the main purpose of business activity.

4 State **two** factors of production for a market trader.

Sample questions

Example 1:
Define 'factor of production'. [2]

Sample answer:
The things needed to make goods and services [1] such as land and labour. [1]

Example 2:
TGA is a leading manufacturer of mobile phones.

Outline **two** ways in which TGA could increase added value. [4]

Sample answer:
Way 1: add new features [1] such as better camera zoom. [1]

Way 2: create a strong brand image [1] so that people are willing to pay more for its phones. [1]

Examination-style questions

NSN makes a range of luxury cars. People like its handmade seats and car warranty. This is a competitive market. The Finance Director knows that resources are scarce, and he must use factors of production carefully. He believes that for every decision he makes, there will be an opportunity cost. The Finance Director is looking for ways to increase added value.

a Define 'opportunity cost'. [2]

b Identify **two** factors of production.
Factor 1:
Factor 2: [2]

c Outline **two** benefits to NSN of increasing added value.
Benefit 1:
Benefit 2: [4]

d Explain **two** ways that NSN could increase added value.
Way 1:
Way 2: [8]

Classification of businesses

Learning summary

By the end of this unit you should understand:

- [ ] the difference between primary, secondary and tertiary sectors

- [ ] reasons for the changing importance of business classification

- [ ] the difference between the private sector and public sector.

2.01 Classification of business

Businesses are grouped into three main types of business activity (sectors):

Primary sector

This involves the **extraction**, growing or collecting of raw materials. Examples include mining, farming and fishing.

Secondary sector

This includes any business involved in assembly, processing or construction. Businesses will either make a finished product or make parts for another business to use. Examples include **manufacturing** and refining.

Tertiary sector

Other businesses need to use **services** such as transport, retailing, warehousing and finance to get products to consumers. Examples of services for individuals include health care, education and restaurants.

Name of sector	Primary	Secondary	Tertiary
Main activity	Extract	Make	Service
Example	Cotton farmer	Clothing factory	Transport company or retailer

Table 2.01 Summary of the three sectors.

TIP Some businesses can be involved in more than one stage of production.

All **three** sectors are linked together. If any part of the chain breaks down, the customer will not get the finished products.

TERMS

Primary sector: businesses that extract or collect raw materials.

Secondary sector: businesses that take raw materials and turn them into finished goods.

Tertiary sector: businesses that provide services to other businesses and individuals.

Sample question

PVN is a printing business in the secondary sector.

Define 'secondary sector'. **[2]**

Sample answer:
It is where things are made. For example, PVN will take wood pulp and use it to make paper.

 TIP You do not need to use a textbook definition as long as you can clearly explain what the term means.

2.02 The changing importance of business classification

The size of each sector varies among different countries. It can also change over time. Reasons for this include:

- Deindustrialisation – there is a decline in manufacturing while the tertiary sector increases.

- Raw materials are discovered/depleted in different countries.

- Specialisation – some countries are good at making certain products or services.

- Some countries have large workforces so can make products at a lower cost.

- Rising living standards – people have more time and money for leisure activities.

Sample question

The employment minister in country C has been looking at some employment data, as shown in Figure 2.01. He said, 'We used to be a country known for growing sugar. Now it's all hotels and shops. What has happened?'

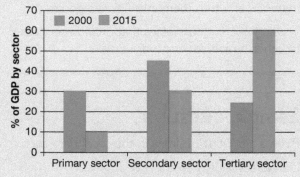

Figure 2.01 Country C percentage of Gross Domestic Product (GDP) by sector.

NOTE: GDP has risen from $500m in 2000 to $700m in 2015.

Identify **two** changes shown by the data in Figure 2.01. For each one, explain a possible reason for the change. **[6]**

Sample answer:

Change 1: Fall in primary sector by 20%. People may have moved to tertiary sector in search of higher wages. **[3]**

Change 2: Fall in secondary sector by 15%. This could be due to the fact that some goods can be made cheaper in other countries. **[3]**

TIP

If you are asked to interpret charts or tables, use the numbers to support your answer.

2.03 The public and private sectors

Most countries have both a public sector and private sector: this is called a mixed economy. Examples of public sector organisations include health care, education, defence, public transport and energy. Sole traders and limited companies are examples of private sector businesses (see 4.01 and 4.04).

TIP

All public and private sector organisations are involved in some form of business activity – it is only the **objectives** (what, for whom and why they produce goods and services) that differ.

TERMS

Public sector: any business owned, run or controlled by the government.

Private sector: any business owned, run or controlled by private individuals.

Public corporation: a business organisation owned and controlled by the government.

Progress check

1 In which sector would you find a public corporation?

2 Give **two** examples of a secondary sector business.

3 Using a ring as an example of a product, show the link between the **three** sectors.

4 What is the difference between public and private sector businesses?

Summary

Businesses can be grouped into three sectors. The importance of each sector for an economy can change. Goods and services can be provided by either public or private sector businesses.

Sample question

Example:
Post Now is a private limited company. It is a letter delivery service in the private sector. Its main competitor, MPO, is in the public sector.

Explain **two** differences between the two businesses. [6]

Sample answer:
Difference 1: Post Now is owned by individuals [1] who bought shares in the private limited company [1], while MPO is owned by the government. [1]

Difference 2: Post Now's objective is to make profit [1] from delivering letters [1] while MPO's priority will be to provide a service. [1]

Examination-style questions

Question 1

Ravel is a farmer in country A. He has been looking at some data, shown in Table 2.02. He cannot understand why there is a difference in employment between countries. Both countries have a mixed economy.

	Country A	Country B
Primary sector	45	10
Secondary sector	20	20
Tertiary	35	70

Table 2.02 Percentage of labour force employed in each country.

NOTE: Population of each country is 60 million.

a Identify **one** type of business that could be found in the:

- primary sector
- secondary sector. [2]

b Calculate the number of people employed in the tertiary sector in country A. [2]

c Explain **two** possible reasons for the difference in the percentage of labour employed in different sectors in each country. [8]

Question 2

SRT makes a wide range of paints. These are sold to businesses and customers in many countries. Market research is important. The Managing Director said, 'Different countries have different legal standards for paint. Customers want different colours and sizes of tins.' SRT uses the services of many businesses from the tertiary sector.

Explain **four** important tertiary sector businesses that SRT might use. [8]

Enterprise, business growth and size

Learning summary

By the end of this unit you should understand:

- ☐ the characteristics of successful entrepreneurs
- ☐ the contents and importance of a business plan
- ☐ the different methods and problems of measuring business size
- ☐ why some businesses grow and others remain small
- ☐ why some businesses fail.

3.01 Characteristics of successful entrepreneurs

Entrepreneurs invest their time, skill and money to set up a business. Anyone can be an entrepreneur if they have the necessary qualities.

Figure 3.01 Characteristics of an entrepreneur.

> **TIP**
> An entrepreneur can be categorised under 'enterprise' in the factors of production (see 1.04).

3.02 How business plans assist entrepreneurs

A business plan can help a business. It can:

- **support loan applications** (for example, a bank is more willing to lend if it can see it is likely to be repaid)
- **give a sense of purpose** and direction so the employees know what to do to achieve the plan
- **help decision-making** so time and resources are not wasted
- **help understand possible risks**, especially if it is a new business.

> **TIP**
> A business plan is not just for new businesses.

> **TERMS**
>
> Entrepreneur: someone who organises, operates and takes the risk for a new business venture.
>
> Business plan: this contains the aims and objectives of a business, and important details about its operations, finance and owners.

- Aims and objectives

- Details about the product

- Market information, for example size of market, customer information, competitors

- How and where product is to be made

- Number and type of employees

- Finance required, cash flow forecasts

Figure 3.02 Main sections of a business plan.

3.03 How and why governments support business start-ups

New businesses can offer many benefits to the economy and consumers.

- Jobs create lower unemployment.

- Increased competition could lead to more choice or lower prices.

- They can provide specialist or new services.

- Start-up businesses, if successful, could grow into **large** businesses.

Governments provide a range of support including:

- financial – grants and subsidies, lower tax rates

- information, advice and support

- location – enterprise zones, rent-free spaces

- training courses for entrepreneurs and/or workers.

3.04 Methods and problems of measuring business size

Small, medium or large business? Size can matter. Being large could indicate business growth or a lower risk for lenders. There is no perfect way to measure size.

Measure	How it is measured	Possible problems with using this measure
Number of employees	Number of employees in the business	What happens if a business uses a lot of machinery? What if it has lots of part-time employees?
Capital employed	Amount of money invested by owners/ borrowed from lenders	Any business can have a lot of expensive machinery, so capital employed is high.
Value of output	Amount of output over a given period	How can this be compared if different types of products are made? What if not all of the products are sold?
Value of sales	Value of sales over a given period	A firm might sell a few high value items while another firm may sell many cheap items.

Table 3.01 Measuring the size of a business organisation.

TIP

Profit is NOT classed as a measure of size. This is because too many factors influence the amount of profit made.

3.05 Why owners may want to expand the business

Growth is an objective for some businesses. Advantages include:

- **Economies of scale** – leading to lower average/unit costs.

- **Diversification/spread risk** – so the business is less reliant on one market or product.

- **Financial reasons** – higher profits, or able to borrow money more easily.

- **Personal objectives** – power and status.

- **Market domination** – increased power or market share in existing markets, so the business can gain more influence with suppliers and customers.

- **Access to new markets.**

3.06 Different ways a business can grow

There are two ways a business can grow: internally and externally.

Method	Internal	External
	By expanding its own activities	By taking over or joining with another business
Advantages	✔ Able to keep control ✔ Relatively inexpensive as business can use own resources	✔ Much quicker so gain benefits of growth faster
Disadvantages	✗ Very slow process	✗ Harder to control ✗ Change of ownership?

Table 3.02 Advantages and disadvantages of internal and external growth.

TinPot makes metal cans for drinks. Let's look at the different ways it might grow in Figure 3.03.

Sample question

Rafa owns a successful jam-making business. He started ten years ago and has made a profit every year. All the jam is sold at local markets. Rafa wants to grow his business. He cannot decide whether to start making sweets or try to find a new market for his jam.

Which method of expansion do you think Rafa should use? Justify your answer. **[6]**

Sample answer:
Rafa has no experience of sweet-making [1] so it will take time to learn these skills [1], and even if he does there is no guarantee of success [1]. He is known for his jam so this reputation can help attract new customers. [1] While sweets might help to spread risk, as he is already successful [1] it would be safer to try to broaden his target market [1].

Internal ways to grow

- make more of current products
- find new markets for current products
- develop new products.

Figure 3.03 Ways TinPot could grow

External ways to grow

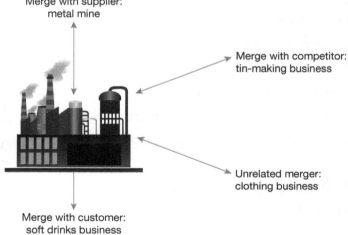

Merge with supplier: metal mine

Merge with competitor: tin-making business

Unrelated merger: clothing business

Merge with customer: soft drinks business

3.07 The problems of growth

Growth (internal or external) does not guarantee success.

Problems of growth	Different options to overcome problems
Harder to manage and control	Hire specialist managers
	Review organisational structure
Communication problems	Use two-way communication methods (see 9.03)
	Delegate and involve employees in decision-making
Financial problems	Use long-term sources of finance (see 19.02)
	Grow at steady rate
Lack of focus	Set clear objectives

Table 3.03 How to overcome problems of growth.

Sample question

ARG is a large food retailer. It has 1200 shops and has 160 000 employees across country A. The Managing Director of ARG plans to take over HBC, which sells electrical goods such as televisions. She said, 'The food market is very competitive. Customer demands and technology are constantly changing. I know many of our stakeholder groups will be affected.' HBC has 800 shops and 47 000 employees.

Explain **one** advantage and **one** disadvantage for ARG's business of taking over HBC. [8]

Sample answer:

Advantage: Spread risk. As it is in a competitive market, ARG's food sales might decline as customers choose rival products. This way, ARG has another market to rely on for revenue. [4]

Disadvantage: Harder for ARG's management to control. The new business will have 2000 shops and 207 000 employees, so it could take much longer for decisions to reach all employees, if at all. As customer demands are constantly changing, ARG might be too slow to react and lose sales to rivals. [4]

3.08 Reasons why some businesses remain small

- Demand in market may not be large enough so it is not possible to grow.
- The business offers specialist goods or services (niche markets).
- Owners want to be their own boss.
- A small business can be more flexible, and able to react to market changes quickly.

3.09 Why some businesses fail

Not all businesses will be successful. Both established and new businesses can and do fail.

New businesses are at higher risk, as they are not established in the market. It can be difficult to persuade customers to try a new product. Owners may lack experience to make the right decisions. Raising finance and cash flow (liquidity problems) are common difficulties.

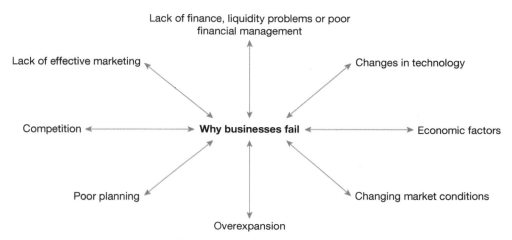

Figure 3.04 Reasons why some businesses fail.

Progress check

1 What does the word 'entrepreneur' mean?

2 Outline **one** problem of using employees as a measure of business size.

3 State **two** ways a business can grow internally.

4 Identify **two** reasons why a business might remain small.

Summary

Entrepreneurs are people who start up new businesses. Governments try to support such businesses. The size of a business can be measured in many ways. Many businesses will want to grow while others remain small.

Sample question

Grace is an entrepreneur. She wants to open a beauty salon in town. She has $400 in savings and some experience from a part-time job. She has read that 80% of new businesses fail. She believes the government will help new business start-ups.

Example 1:
Identify **two** reasons why new businesses might fail. **[2]**

Sample answer:
Reason 1: Lack of cash flow. **[1]**

Reason 2: Wrong location. **[1]**

TIP
This is a generic question so a simple list of possible reasons is acceptable for this type of question.

Sample questions

Example 2:
Explain **two** characteristics Grace needs to be a successful entrepreneur. **[6]**

Sample answer:
Characteristic 1: Risk-taker **[1]**: 80% of new businesses fail; **[1]** so she must be prepared to lose all her savings **[1]**.

Characteristic 2: Effective communicator **[1]**: as beauty salon is a service; **[1]** she needs to encourage people to return **[1]**.

Example 3:
Explain **two** ways in which a government might help Grace's business. **[6]**

Sample answer:
Way 1: Financial support **[1]**: Grace only has $400 **[1]** and is likely to have high start-up costs **[1]**.

Way 2: Advice **[1]** to help make better decisions **[1]** as she only has some experience **[1]**.

TIP
If a question **asks for a decision, make one**. Either viewpoint is acceptable as long as it is then supported by your answer.

Examination-style questions

Glass Brothers (GB) is a successful small glass-making business. It is a business partnership owned by two brothers, Kai and Kit. GB makes a range of products from windows to bottles, in an old factory near the city centre. Kai has been looking at GB's business plan. He wants to grow the business but cannot decide the best method to use. Kit, the Production manager, wants to develop new products. A local window-fitting business has offered to join the two businesses together.

a   Identify **two** ways to measure the size of a business.
    Way 1:
    Way 2:   [2]

b   Outline **two** possible benefits to GB of having a business plan.
    Benefit 1:
    Benefit 2:   [4]

c   Explain **two** possible problems for GB's business if it grows too large.
    Problem 1:
    Problem 2:   [8]

d   State the advantages and disadvantages to GB of the following **two** methods of growth. Which method do you think GB should use? Justify your answer.
    Join with another business:
    Expand its product range:
    Recommendation: [12]

Types of business organisation

Learning summary

By the end of this unit you should understand:

- ■ the main features of different forms of business organisation

- ■ the difference between unincorporated and limited companies

- ■ concepts of risk, ownership and limited liability

- ■ business organisations in the public sector.

Private sector businesses can be classed into four main forms, based on their legal structure:

- sole traders

- partnerships

- private limited companies

- public limited companies.

TIP

Focus on the features and differences of each type of business. You do not need to know the details about how they are set up.

TIP

'Sole' only refers to one owner. The business can have many employees.

TERMS

Partnership: a business owned and controlled by two or more people.

Sole trader: a business owned and controlled by one person.

4.01 Sole trader

- One person owns and controls the business.

- This is the most common form of business.

- It is an unincorporated business – the owner does not have a separate legal identity.

- Examples: carpenter, hairdresser, local stall owner.

Advantages	Disadvantages
• Can make decisions quickly	• Unlimited liability
• Easy to set up	• Limited sources of finance
• Keep all the profit	• No one to share workload with
• Business details are private	• Only have own skills and ideas to rely on
• Total control	• Carry all business risks

Table 4.01 Advantages and disadvantages of being a sole trader.

4.02 Partnerships

- Each partner has an equal say in how the business is run, in return for an equal (or agreed) share of the profits.

- It is an unincorporated business.

- Examples: doctors, accountants.

Advantages	Disadvantages
• Can share workload and ideas	• Usually unlimited liability
• Partner can cover if other owner(s) ill or away	• Limited sources of finance
• More sources of finance than sole trader	• Must share profits
• Business details are private	• Slower decision-making than sole trader
• Partners can specialise in tasks	• Disagreements can cause problems
• Share risk and responsibilities	• Everyone responsible for actions of other partners

Table 4.02 Advantages and disadvantages of partnerships.

4.03 The difference between unincorporated businesses and limited companies

- Sole traders and partnerships (both unincorporated) have unlimited liability.

The owner is responsible for all the debts of the business. If the business fails, the owner can be forced to sell personal possessions to repay any business debts.

- Limited companies have limited liability.

These businesses have a separate identity from their owners. Owners can only lose the money invested in the business, and their personal assets are safe. This can encourage more investment, as risk is limited to the amount invested.

4.04 What is a limited company?

- This is an incorporated business – the business is responsible for its own debts.
- It is run by directors who do not need to be shareholders.
- Owners have limited liability – they are only liable for the debts of the business up to the amount invested.
- Shareholders have no responsibility for day-to-day decisions.

TIP

The difference between a **public limited company** and a **private limited company** focuses on who can own them and how its shares are sold.

TERMS

Shareholder: any individual or organisation that owns shares in a business.

Incorporated business: a business that exists separately from its owners.

Unincorporated business: the owners do not have a separate legal identity.

Limited liability: owners are only liable for the amount invested in a business.

4.05 Private limited companies

- 'Private' means that shares can only be sold if all shareholders agree.
- Shares are a unit of ownership. Each one represents an equal part of a company's capital.
- Shares tend to be owned by family and friends.

Advantages	Disadvantages
• Limited liability	• Expensive to set up
• Can raise additional finance by selling shares	• Restricted number of shareholders could limit amount possible to raise
• Easier to keep control compared to public limited company	• Need agreement of other shareholders to sell shares
• Incorporated	• Cannot sell shares on Stock Exchange
• Continuity of existence	• Must disclose some financial information

Table 4.03 Advantages and disadvantages of private limited companies.

4.06 Public limited companies

- Anyone can own shares in a public limited company.
- This kind of business can raise vast amounts of money by selling shares to anyone.
- Shareholders vote for directors at the Annual General Meeting.

Advantages	Disadvantages
• Limited liability	• Very expensive to set up
• Able to raise very large amounts of finance to fund expansion	• Must disclose detailed financial information every year
• Able to sell shares on Stock Exchange	• Additional costs of advertising/selling shares on Stock Exchange
• Do not need other shareholders' permission to sell shares	• Individual shareholders have little say in how business runs
• Incorporated	• Greater risk of takeover as cannot control who buys shares
• Continuity of existence	

Table 4.04 Advantages and disadvantages of public limited companies.

 TIP Public limited companies are in the private sector. 'Public' just means that anyone can buy the shares.

TERMS

Private limited company: a business whose shares cannot be sold to the general public.

Public limited company: a business whose shares can be freely bought and sold to the general public.

Sample question

Alejandro is an accountant in a large company. He wants to set up his own accountancy business. He has a few customers arranged. His sister, Miranda, has offered to become his business partner. As a new business advisor in a local bank, she knows the problems of running a small business. She has already found rent-free premises for the office. Alejandro cannot decide on which is the best type of business organisation to choose.

Consider the advantages and disadvantages of the following **three** options for Alejandro.

- sole trader
- partnership
- private limited company

Which option do you think Alejandro should choose? Justify your answer. **[12]**

Sample answer:
Sole trader: Alejandro has already worked for a large business so this time he might not want to take orders or listen to someone else. As his own boss he would have total control. However, the risk of starting up on his own could damage his chances of survival.

Partnership: Alejandro will have someone to share the workload with. His sister could manage the office, something she knows a lot about. This will give Alejandro more time to focus on accounts. This could help create a better customer service, which could help increase his reputation and attract additional customers.

Private limited company: This is not a good idea. It is harder to set up, as there are more forms to fill in. He might get more money from investors and have limited liability but it is not really used by a new business.

Conclusion: The best option for Alejandro is a partnership. He will have to share control with his sister but does not have to do everything himself. He can use her knowledge from the bank to benefit the business. While he would still have unlimited liability and risk losing his personal assets, they both have relevant knowledge to offset this.

TIP

Do not just list knowledge points. Try to develop points identified to help answer the set question.

4.07 Franchises and joint ventures

- A franchisee pays to buy the rights to sell a product, in return for a known product, marketing material and business support.

- A franchisor is the business which allows the franchisee the right to sell its products or services.

- Examples: McDonald's, KFC.

Franchisee

Advantages	Disadvantages
• More chance of success, as selling a well-known product	• Less independence than sole trader as some rules set by franchisor
• Banks more likely to lend money as the risk is lower than a new business	• Cannot keep all the profit
• Has support of franchisor – advice, training and marketing	• Can only sell products of the franchisor
• Success of another franchisee can help own franchise	• Has little or no choice of suppliers to lower costs

Table 4.05 Advantages and disadvantages of being a franchisee.

Franchisor

Advantages	Disadvantages
• Expand business without investing large amounts of money	• One bad franchisee can ruin reputation of the whole company
• Risks shared with franchisee	• Costs of supporting all franchisees
• Receive regular royalty payments	• Only gets a set percentage of profit made. If successful do not gain all the profit
• Most franchisees are more motivated so greater chance of profit	

Table 4.06 Advantages and disadvantages of being a franchisor.

TERMS

Franchise: an agreement that allows one business to trade under the name of another business to sell the other company's products or services.

Joint venture: an enterprise undertaken by two or more businesses pooling resources together on a specific project.

Joint ventures

- Each business remains separate from each other.

- Joint ventures are used in business expansion, development of new products or moving into new markets.

Advantages	Disadvantages
• Access to new markets	• Unclear communication of objectives
• Access to other established markets and distribution channels	• Objectives of two companies could clash, reducing chances of success
• Less risk as business shares costs with other business	• Have to share profits
• Access to new technology, expertise and knowledge	• Different cultures and management styles so could be lack of leadership
• Increased capacity	• Disagreements possible if one party provides more expertise or finance than other

Table 4.07 Advantages and disadvantages of being a franchisor.

TIP

A joint venture is different to a merger. In a joint venture, businesses work together on a specific project. They remain separate businesses, unlike a merger.

4.08 Public corporations

- This is a business owned and controlled by the government.
- It is financed by government through taxation.
- It aims to provide services to people at low or no cost.
- Examples: hospitals and schools.

TIP Public corporations do not have to make a profit.

4.09 Relationship between risk, ownership and limited liability

Progress check

1 Outline the main difference in ownership between a sole trader and partnership.
2 Why can unlimited liability be a problem for some businesses?
3 Define 'a franchise'.
4 What is the difference between a joint venture and a merger?

Summary

There are many forms of organisation. Each has implications for ownership, control and risk. The form chosen will also help determine how easy it is for the business to access finance.

Type of business	Control	Main objective	Risk	Liability	Main source of funds
Sole trader	One owner	Profit, Survival, Growth	All with owner	Unlimited	Own funds, Loans
Partnership	Shared between partners	Profit, Survival, Growth	Shared by partners	Unlimited	Partners' funds, Loans
Private limited company	Delegated by owners to directors	Profit, Growth	Limited to investment	Limited	Share capital, Loans
Public limited company	Delegated by owners to directors	Profit, Growth	Limited to investment	Limited	Share capital, Loans

Table 4.08 Relationship between risk, ownership and limited liability.

Sample questions

Abraham is a car mechanic. He has always wanted to run his own business. He has $15000 in savings. Abraham has researched two options. For either option he will need to find the right location.

Option 1: Start a new car repair business as a sole trader. He will need to borrow an additional $10000 to buy equipment.

Option 2: Buy a franchise for QFIX cars, the leading repair company in the country. He will need $50000 to buy the franchise, in addition to $10000 for equipment. All QFIX franchisees receive full training, and marketing support.

Example 1:
Which option do you think Abraham should choose? Justify your answer. [6]

Sample answer:
Franchise – Business failure is less likely as customers are more likely to trust [1] a leading car repair business [1]. Marketing will be done for him so this lowers cost [1]. This can help cash flow, which can be a problem for a new business [1]. Even though less independent, he still makes some decisions [1]. There is more chance of success as so much support is available to get established [1].

Example 2:
Explain **two** advantages to QFIX cars of selling franchises. [8]

Sample answer:
Advantage 1: Cheaper way to expand [1]; franchisee pays $50000 [1] so QFIX will not spend large amounts of its finance [1] to increase its garage business [1].

Advantage 2: Keep control over image [1] of repair services offered [1], as Abraham must follow rules set by QFIX [1], so QFIX should be able to retain its reputation as a leading business [1].

Examination-style questions

Kallis Engineering (KE) is a private limited company. It is a small engineering business based in South Africa. It makes farm equipment including tractors and trailers. The Finance Director wants to raise an additional $20m in finance as KE plans to expand by selling its equipment in Asia. She said, 'This is a very competitive market, but with the right marketing strategy I think this can work.' She also knows there are benefits of trading overseas. KE are considering changing the business into a public limited company. She cannot decide whether to use debt or equity to raise the finance.

a   Define 'private limited company'.   [2]

b   Define 'limited liability'.   [2]

c   Explain **two** advantages to KE of being a private limited company.

   Advantage 1:

   Advantage 2:   [8]

d   Consider the advantages and disadvantages of the following **two** forms of business organisation for KE. Which form do you think KE should choose? Justify your answer.

   Private limited company:

   Public limited company:

   Recommendation: [12]

Business objectives and stakeholder objectives

5.01 Why businesses need objectives

Objectives act as a target for a business. Objectives will vary and change, depending on factors such as size, type of business, economic situation and differing aims of stakeholders.

Objectives are important to provide direction, and act as a measure against which to judge success.

Most private sector businesses have the same main objectives:

* profit
* survival/break-even
* increasing sales revenue
* increasing market share
* growth.

Other objectives include:

* providing quality products/service
* customer satisfaction
* social, ethical and environmental responsibilities.

TERM

Objective: a target that a business wants to reach so it can achieve its aims.

Sample question

RLP makes computers. The Managing Director's objective is to increase market share by 5% in each of the next four years. He is thinking of taking over one of RLP's competitors.

Explain **two** benefits to RLP of setting objectives. **[6]**

Sample answer:
Benefit 1: Measure of success: if RLP achieves the 5% increase in market share, they will know that it has been a good few years. **[3]**

Benefit 2: Aid to decision-making as RLP will be able to see if taking over its rival will help achieve its goal. **[3]**

5.02 Social enterprise

This is a business that puts social objectives ahead of financial objectives. Any profits made are reinvested back into the business or community to benefit others.

Examples include:

* Open a bakery/restaurant that focuses on building employment skills for underemployed groups.
* Create a food market that sells food to low income communities at a discounted price.
* Build a new kind of consumer electronic device, built with conflict-free materials, and provide fair wages (pay) to the employees who build it.

5.03 Different stakeholders and their objectives

Business activity has an impact on many people both **inside** (internal stakeholder) and **outside** (external stakeholder) the business.

Internal stakeholder group	Typical objectives	Possible influence
Shareholders	• Increased dividends from profits • Rise in value of shares	• Power to vote out directors • Sell off or refuse to buy additional shares
Employees (includes managers)	• Good working conditions • Better pay • Job security • Success leading to promotion • Status and power	• Take industrial action • Affect quality or quantity of products if do not work hard • Leave job • Managers in charge of day-to-day activities, so some control over actions

Table 5.01 Objectives and influence of internal stakeholder groups.

External stakeholder group	Typical objectives	Possible influence
Customers	• High quality products • Good customer service • Competitive prices	• Stop buying goods • Write bad reviews
Banks and other lenders	• Want business that can afford to pay back loans • Good return on investment	• Can demand money back • Refuse to lend money
Local community	• Social/environmental issues such as jobs, less pollution, available local services	• Organise pressure groups to influence business or government
Government	• Economic growth • Increased employment • Protection of employees and customers	• Legislation • Financial support • Government policies
Suppliers	• Increase sales volume • Regular payments	• Can withdraw supplies or trade credit

Table 5.02 Objectives and influence of external stakeholder groups.

Conflicts are inevitable. For example:

- More pay for employees can result in less profit available for shareholder dividends.

- Higher levels of output could lead to more jobs and pollution for the community.

Summary

You need to understand what objectives are, and why they are important to a business. Remember that different types of business organisation will have different objectives. These objectives will change, depending on the stakeholders and current situation of the business.

Sample question

Paolo owns a small music shop. He specialises in selling and repairing guitars and violins. Paolo plans to increase prices.

Outline how Paolo's objectives might clash with those of his customers. [4]

Sample answer:
As Paolo wants to increase profit, he could charge higher prices. Customers will want more choice and lower prices. They will not want to pay more for his guitars, but if there is no alternative, they might have to pay, even if they cannot afford it.

5.04 Objectives of private and public sector enterprises

	Public sector	**Private sector**
Definition	Any business owned, run or controlled by the government	Any business owned, run or controlled by private individuals
Examples	Health care, education, police force	Sole trader, limited companies and partnership businesses
Typical objectives	• Provide a service • Control natural monopolies • Protect key industries	• Profit • Growth • Market share • Sales revenue
Aim to benefit	Everyone	Individual owners

Table 5.03 Objectives of private and public sector enterprises.

Progress check

1 How can objectives help a business?

2 How do the aims of a social enterprise differ from those of private sector firms?

3 Explain **one** possible objective for a new business.

4 Identify **two** objectives of a public sector business.

Sample questions

TUP is a private limited company. One of its objectives is profit. TUP makes low-cost building blocks from recycling waste plastic. TUP rents an old factory near the city centre. Materials are delivered most days. Demand has increased quickly from 1000 to 25 000 blocks per week. The Production manager is worried about protests from pressure groups concerned about increased pollution. She says, 'TUP creates many externalities. I need deliveries every day now, as well as 30 more employees. TUP may need a new site!' She believes most stakeholders will benefit from the increase in production.

Example 1:
Explain how the following **three** stakeholders are likely to be affected by increases in production:

• shareholders

• employees

• community

Which stakeholder do you think will benefit the most? Justify your answer. [12]

Sample answer:
Shareholders: Shareholders will benefit greatly as TUP increases its profit when more blocks sold [1], so they will benefit from receiving a higher dividend [1]. Also value of the shares will increase, so they will receive more if they sell their shares [1].

Employees: Employees will benefit from increased job security [1] as orders have increased significantly and could benefit with higher wages based on the extra work [1]. There is a risk of being overworked as 25 000 blocks is a significant increase [1] and it could take time to find the 30 extra workers. This could demotivate employees [1].

Community: The benefit will depend on when and how many deliveries, and whether fumes add to pollution and damage people's health [1]. If the factory moves to a new site, damage to public health will already have been done, so this is a negative effect [1].

Conclusion: The community is likely to benefit the least, as the risk of negative externalities will offset any potential benefits [1]. Shareholders will benefit in the long term as profits (and possible dividends) could rise as production increases. However in the short term, profits may be lower if funds are needed to cover any costs of

expansion especially as there are concerns about pollution, which could limit potential returns [1]. Employees should benefit the most as extra work and more jobs being available should increase both job security and potentially wages, whereas how much shareholders benefit will depend on the amount of profit made [1].

Example 2:
Identify **two** objectives (other than profit) that TUP might have. **[2]**

Sample answer:
Objective 1: Social responsibility. [1]

Objective 2: Growth. [1]

TIP Always read the question carefully to ensure that you have the right focus in your answer.

Examination-style questions

ARG is a large food retailer. It has 1200 shops and 160 000 employees across country A. The Managing Director plans to take over HBC, which sells electrical goods such as televisions. She said, 'This is a very competitive market. Customer demands and technology are constantly changing. I know many of our stakeholder groups will be affected.' HBC has 800 shops and 47 000 employees.

a Define 'stakeholder group'. [2]

b Identify **two** possible objectives ARG could set.
Objective 1:
Objective 2: [2]

c ARG is in the private sector. Explain **two** ways in which the objectives might be different if the business was owned by the government.
Way 1:
Way 2: [8]

d Identify **two** stakeholder groups, and explain why each group is important to ARG.
Stakeholder group 1:
Stakeholder group 2: [6]

Section 2:
PEOPLE IN BUSINESS

Motivating employees

6.01 Why people work

People work to satisfy human needs:

- **Money** – people need money to pay for their needs and wants.
- **Security** – having a job that will be there for many years.
- **Job satisfaction** – enjoying what they do.
- **Self-esteem** – feeling important as they have something to contribute to society.
- **Social** – feeling part of a group and having friends.

6.02 The concept of motivation

Everyone works for different reasons. A business has to offer the right rewards to suit each individual, in order to encourage them to work harder.

Motivated employees are likely to:

- be more productive
- produce better quality work
- contribute more ideas
- be loyal and have a lower rate of absenteeism.

This could help the business achieve:

↑ more sales

↑ more efficient production

↓ lower costs

↑ more profit.

TIP

'Retention' means that the employees stay at the business. This is a good thing, as the business has to spend less time and money in recruiting new employees. When there is poor retention of employees, quality and output can be negatively affected.

TERM

Motivation: the factor that makes people want to do something.

6.03 Key motivational theories

Each theory tries to explain what motivates different people. This should help the business choose the right reward to increase employees' motivation.

TIP

You will not be asked to explain any of the theories in detail. Learn the key features of each and how a business can use it.

Maslow's Hierarchy of Needs

This is based on the idea that everyone is motivated by the same things (needs). To motivate people, each set of needs must be satisfied in the right order; once achieved, it no longer acts as a motivator.

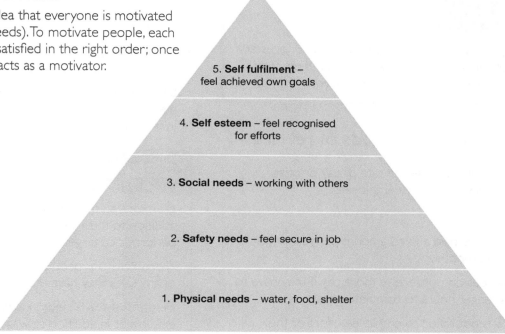

5. **Self fulfilment** – feel achieved own goals

4. **Self esteem** – feel recognised for efforts

3. **Social needs** – working with others

2. **Safety needs** – feel secure in job

1. **Physical needs** – water, food, shelter

Figure 6.01 Maslow's Hierarchy of Needs.

Level	This means	How is this achieved
5 Self fulfilment	Achieved own goals	Help employees set and reach personal targets
4 Self esteem	Feel recognised for efforts	Use praise/reward good work/opportunities for promotion
3 Social needs	Work and mix with others	Encourage team work
2 Safety needs	Feel safe and secure	Provide job security and better working conditions
1 Physical needs	Water, food, shelter	Paid for by basic wage

Table 6.01 The levels in Maslow's Hierarchy of Needs.

Taylor's Scientific Management

1 Taylor assumed that money was the main motivator for employees.

2 He divided jobs into simple steps to work out how much could be produced each day. Employees are trained to do specific jobs in the process. Managers supervise the work.

3 Pay is based on the number of items made – **piece rate**. This should increase productivity.

4 Problems – work is repetitive, leading to boredom. Money is only one factor in motivation. This theory will not work for all jobs.

Herzberg's hygiene factors

Herzberg believed that employees' needs could be split into two groups.

Hygiene factors	Motivating factors
• Factors necessary for people to work, but do not make people work harder.	• Factors which encourage people to work harder.
This means:	This means:
• Employees expect basic and safety needs to be provided for them. • These factors do not motivate employees.	• Adding variety/tasks can make work more interesting. • Sharing responsibility, consulting and praising employees are good ways to motivate.

Table 6.02 Herzberg's hygiene factors.

Hygiene factor: any factors which are necessary for people to work, but do not make them work harder (such as basic and safety needs).

6.04 Financial methods of rewards

A business can increase the rate of pay or offer additional payments to its employees.

Salary

Employees are paid a fixed amount per year, which is usually paid monthly.

✓ Employees do not receive more pay if they have to work longer hours to complete a task.

✗ Salary is not linked to employee effort or the amount produced.

Time rate

Employees are paid a set amount for each hour worked. This is a useful method when it is difficult to measure output.

✓ Time rate can encourage people to work for longer.

✗ It can also lead to a slow rate of work.

Piece rate

Employees are paid by the amount of output they produce.

✓ This encourages employees to produce more and work quicker.

✗ It can lead to poor quality, as employees might rush.

Fringe benefits

These are extra incentives given in addition to wages. Examples include discounts on products, insurance or a company car.

Performance-related pay

Pay is based on an assessment of how well someone is doing the job. This can take many forms.

- **Bonuses** – employees receive extra money above basic pay if they reach certain performance targets.

- **Commission** – salespeople are given an incentive to sell more as they receive a percentage of any sales made.

- **Profit sharing** – additional payments are based on the level of business profits.

- **Share ownership** – in limited companies, employees have a chance to buy shares to become part owners in the business. They can receive dividends.

TERMS

Bonus: a sum of money paid to employees, in addition to their basic pay, if they reach certain performance targets.

Commission: people earn a certain percentage of any sales they have made.

Fringe benefits: extra incentives given to employees in addition to wages.

Profit sharing: employees receive an additional payment based on the level of business profits.

Sample question

CWB makes a range of pottery including plates and cups. The company has a reputation for quality. All employees are paid by piece rate. The Operations manager is looking for ways to improve employees' motivation.

Explain **one** advantage and **one** disadvantage to CWB of using piece rate. **[6]**

Sample answer:
Advantage: Encourages high output, so more pottery is available for sale: increased output means that extra goods can be sold. **[3]**

Disadvantage: Encourages speed, so this could lead to more mistakes which could damage quality image. **[3]**

6.05 Non-financial methods of rewards

A business cannot afford to pay employees as much as some people want. Also, money does not motivate everyone. Good communication and involving employees in decision-making can be just as effective in motivating employees. Training and opportunities for promotion are also factors that can affect employee motivation. Having more challenging or varied work can make employees feel valued. Examples include:

- job enrichment
- job rotation
- job enlargement
- team working.

Job enrichment

The employee is given more responsibility or more difficult tasks to do.

Advantages	Disadvantages
• Less supervision is needed. • Reduces boredom as work is more challenging. • Develops employees' skills.	• Employees might need training which adds to costs. • Employees might want a pay rise.

Table 6.03 Advantages and disadvantages of job enrichment.

Job rotation

Employees do one simple job for a period, and then move to another simple job.

Advantages	Disadvantages
• Creates a flexible workforce as employees are able to cover other jobs. • Reduces boredom as there is change between tasks. • Develops employees' skills.	• The range of tasks given are similar, so boredom can return. • Some employees might be better at certain tasks than others. This means that quality and productivity might vary.

Table 6.04 Advantages and disadvantages of job rotation.

Job enlargement

The employee is given extra tasks to do as part of their usual job. The work should be more interesting.

Advantages	Disadvantages
• Reduces boredom as there is more variety of tasks. • Develops employees' skills.	• If the work is just more of the same, the employee could feel they are being overworked.

Table 6.05 Advantages and disadvantages of job enlargement.

Team working

Groups of employees are given responsibility for parts of the production process.

This is often used as part of lean production.

Advantages	Disadvantages
• Less supervision is needed. • Reduces boredom as involvement is encouraged. • Develops employees' skills.	• Employees might need training which adds to costs. • Employees might want a pay rise as they have more responsibility.

Table 6.06 Advantages and disadvantages of team working.

TIP

Most methods will cost money. A business will hope that the extra output or efficiency gained will more than cover the additional costs.

Choosing the right incentive depends on:

- **Cost** – the business needs to be able to afford to give bonuses or pay rises.
- **Type of business** – piece rate might not be suitable for all businesses.
- **Employees** – everyone is an individual. What works for one person may not work for all.
- **Manager** – their skills and choices will affect the success of any method.

Sample question

Colley's sells a wide range of clothes for men and women. The shop employs 30 part-time shop workers, two supervisors and one manager. All employees are paid by time rate. The manager believes that improving motivation can help Colley's increase its sales.

Explain **two** methods Colley's could use to improve motivation. [6]

Sample answer:

Method 1: Commission – employees have an incentive to sell more clothes as they earn more money. [3]

Method 2: Job rotation – employees could switch between men's and women's department so that they do not become bored. [3]

TIP

To support your analysis, do not simply repeat the question; for example, don't say 'this will improve motivation'. Explain how or why the method chosen will do this.

Summary

There are many different theories of motivation and ways of rewarding employees. You need to be able to explain how each method can help increase employees' motivation. Different methods are useful in different situations.

Progress check

1 Why does a business want motivated employees?

2 Name **two** hygiene factors.

3 State the **five** levels in Maslow's hierarchy of needs.

4 What is the difference between commission and piece rate?

Sample questions

MetalKings (MK) is a large mining company. It has 1200 employees. The Human Resources manager is concerned as many people are leaving. She said, 'I don't understand why motivation is poor. Demand for coal is high. Employees are paid above the minimum wage. We offer bonuses and give them safety equipment to use.'

Example 1:
Identify **two** reasons why people work. [2]

Sample answer:
Reason 1: money.

Reason 2: meet other people.

Example 2:
Outline **two** reasons why poor motivation might be a problem for MK. [4]

Sample answer:
Reason 1: lower output [1] so the company is not able to meet the demand for coal [1].

Reason 2: higher recruitment costs [1] as so many people leave [1].

Examination-style questions

Splash Active (SA) specialises in providing activity holidays for families. SA prides itself on its good reputation and competitive prices. The business has won awards for its good customer service and health and safety. SA's organisational structure has a wide span of control and a short chain of command. Employees are seen as an important factor in its success. Few employees leave. All employees are paid by time rate. All managers have a democratic leadership style. Most managers think that praise is the best way to motivate employees.

a   Outline **two** non-financial methods (other than praise) SA could use to motivate its employees.
    Method 1:
    Method 2:   [4]

b   Do you think praise is the best way for SA to motivate its employees? Justify your answer.   [6]

c   Explain **one** advantage and **one** disadvantage to SA of using time rate.
    Advantage:
    Disadvantage: [8]

d   Consider the advantages and disadvantages of the following **three** options that SA could use to reward employees. Which option do you think SA should choose? Justify your answer.
    Bonuses:
    Job enrichment:
    Fringe benefits:
    Conclusion: [12]

Organisation and management

Learning summary

By the end of this chapter you should understand:

- [ ] the main features of simple organisational structures
- [ ] the roles, responsibilities and interrelationships of people within organisations
- [ ] the role of management
- [ ] the main features of different leadership styles
- [ ] the effects of employees being members of a trade union.

7.01 Organisational structure

An organisational structure shows the working relationship between different sections and who is in charge. It is a useful tool as it:

- makes it easy to see everyone's role in the organisation
- shows formal lines of communication so people know who to speak to if there is a problem.

> **TERM**
>
> Organisational structure: a framework that shows how authority and management roles are shared out in a business.

By function

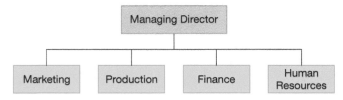

Figure 7.01 A structure organised by function.

- → Each department is organised by task.
- → This is a common structure for limited companies.
- ✓ There is an opportunity for people to specialise in tasks, so they are more productive.
- ✗ There is a possibility of conflict as departments might not work together.

By product

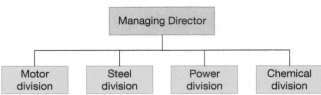

Figure 7.02 A structure organised by product.

- → All products have their own production, marketing and finance departments.
- ✓ If the business has a wide range of products, managers make decisions to suit individual products.
- ✗ This can be expensive as each division has similar functions.

By region

Figure 7.03 A structure organised by region.

- → This structure is common in multinational companies.
- → It is a decentralised structure – authority is delegated to the regions.
- ✓ Managers can focus on their own region, so they are able to react better and more quickly to issues.

✓ This structure improves motivation as employees feel involved in decision-making.

✗ It can be expensive as each division has similar functions in different locations.

✗ Misunderstandings of control and coordination problems can arise if senior managers are not aware of decisions taken elsewhere in the business.

> **TIP**
> You can be asked to draw or interpret an organisational chart, so make sure you know and understand the key features.

> **TIP**
> Sole traders usually have no or very few employees, so there is no need for an organisational chart.

7.02 Main features of organisational structures

Levels of hierarchy

The levels of hierarchy show the number of levels of management: for example, Managing Director, manager, supervisor, production workers.

- Tall organisations have many levels of management.
- Flat organisations have few levels of management.

Chain of command

This shows who makes decisions, and who is responsible for whom.

- The chain of command can be short (few levels) or long (many levels).
- A long chain means slower communications. Messages can become distorted and the wrong actions taken. People at the end of chain can feel isolated, which damages morale.

Span of control

A **wide** span of control means that a manager is responsible for many employees.

Advantages	Disadvantages
• Delegation helps to motivate employees.	• Fewer opportunities for promotion as there are fewer supervisory roles.
• Faster decision-making.	• It is more difficult to control large numbers of employees.
• Communication is quicker and more efficient.	• It is more difficult to know what every subordinate is doing.

Table 7.01 Advantages and disadvantages of a wide span of control.

A **narrow span** of control means that a manager is responsible for few employees.

Advantages	Disadvantages
• Easier to control a small number of employees.	• Employees can feel out of touch with decision-makers.
• The manager will be able to maintain better working relationship with employees.	• Communication problems can arise as there are too many levels for information to pass through.
• More opportunities for employees to be given responsibility or promotion.	• There can be slower decision-making.
• More effective feedback is available.	• Senior management might be less in touch with what is happening in the organisation.

Table 7.02 Advantages and disadvantages of a narrow span of control.

Is a wide or narrow span of control better?

There is no perfect answer. It depends on many factors including:

- **Size of organisation** – a business with few employees might not need much of a hierarchy.
- **Skills of the employees** – highly skilled employees might need less supervision than unskilled employees.
- **Skill and style of manager** – are they willing or able to delegate?
- **Type of work** – simple tasks need less supervision, so a wider span possible.

Organisation 1

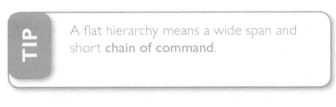

Flat hierarchy: few levels of authority

MD

Manager   Manager

Short chain of command as three levels in hierarchy

Wide span of control – as person is responsible for many employees (six in the example)

Figure 7.04 Example of an organisation with a flat hierarchy.

TIP

A flat hierarchy means a wide span and short **chain of command**.

Organisation 2

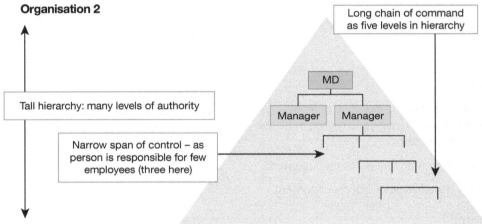

Long chain of command as five levels in hierarchy

Tall hierarchy: many levels of authority

MD

Manager   Manager

Narrow span of control – as person is responsible for few employees (three here)

Figure 7.05 Example of an organisation with a tall hierarchy.

TIP

A tall **hierarchy** means a narrow span and long chain of command.

One way in which a business could try to lower costs is to remove a layer of management in the hierarchy. This is called 'delayering'.

Centralised or decentralised?

- In a centralised organisation, higher levels of management take most decisions.

- Decentralised structures use a lot of delegation, which can speed up decision-making.

The structure can change as a business grows. Most firms start with a centralised structure. Some change to a decentralised structure as the business becomes larger, to avoid control and communication problems.

TERMS

Chain of command: the formal line through which decisions are passed from higher levels of management down the organisation.

Hierarchy: the number of levels of authority in an organisation.

Span of control: the number of subordinates who report directly to a manager.

7.03 The roles, responsibilities and interrelationships between people in organisations

- Each level in the structure has a different level of authority (power).
- Roles at the top of the organisation have more authority and responsibilities than those at the bottom.

7.04 Role of management

Managers have many responsibilities. They have to make decisions, solve problems and deal with people.

Main functions

- **Planning** – set targets and decide what is the best way to achieve them.
- **Organising** – give orders or delegate tasks to appropriate employees. Check the right resources are available.
- **Command** – motivate, communicate, guide and encourage, as well as give orders.
- **Coordinate** – communicate, supervise and give direction to subordinates.
- **Control** – set standards and make sure everything is done correctly and on time.

7.05 Delegation

A manager cannot do everything. Delegation requires managers to trust employees. This reduces the amount of direct control which a manager has.

> **TERM**
>
> Delegation: when a manager gives authority to carry out tasks and make decisions to a subordinate.

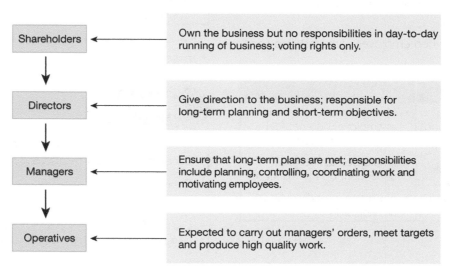

Figure 7.07 Roles and responsibilities within an organisational structure.

Shareholders → Own the business but no responsibilities in day-to-day running of business; voting rights only.

Directors → Give direction to the business; responsible for long-term planning and short-term objectives.

Managers → Ensure that long-term plans are met; responsibilities include planning, controlling, coordinating work and motivating employees.

Operatives → Expected to carry out managers' orders, meet targets and produce high quality work.

The amount of delegation depends on:

- **Organisational structure:** the more tasks a manager delegates, the broader their span of control.

- **Leadership style:** an autocratic manager is less likely to delegate tasks than a democratic manager (see 7.06).

Advantages	Disadvantages
• Saves time for management to do other important jobs.	• Managers are still responsible for any mistakes made.
• Opportunities for employees to learn new skills, which could lead to promotion.	• Time spent explaining tasks can cause delays.
• Work is likely to be more interesting for employees, improving their motivation.	• Managers might feel threatened by good employees, affecting their working relationships.
• It can speed up decision-making.	• Managers might not know what is happening.

Table 7.03 Advantages and disadvantages of delegation.

7.06 The different styles of leadership

There are three main styles – **autocratic, democratic** and **laissez-faire**. Most managers will use only one approach. Some can change their style to suit different situations.

Autocratic

- Manager has total control.

- There is no delegation.

- Communication is one way, from the top downwards.

- This style is used when employees are unskilled (or not trusted).

Advantages	Disadvantages
• The manager feels in control of all situations.	• Motivation can be a problem as employees do not feel involved in decisions.
• Quick decision-making.	• Employees can be too dependent on the manager.
• Employees have clear direction, and they know what to do and expect.	• No scope for individuals to develop skills.

Table 7.04 Advantages and disadvantages of autocratic management.

Democratic

- A democratic manager needs to be a good communicator and willing to delegate.

- This style is useful when employees are skilled and experienced.

Advantages	Disadvantages
• Managers can feel that decisions have the support of employees.	• Decision-making can be slow.
• Employees are likely to be motivated as their views are listened to.	• Problems can arise if employees do not have enough knowledge or experience to make decisions.
• This style encourages loyalty as it gives responsibility to the employee.	• The manager might not agree with the decision but has to accept it.
	• This style can lead to conflict if views differ.

Table 7.05 Advantages and disadvantages of democratic management.

Laissez-faire

- Managers have little influence in the actions of the employees.

- The manager is only involved in resolving disagreements.

- This style is good for small, highly motivated teams.

Advantages	Disadvantages
• People can be more motivated as they are free to do what they think best.	• There is no real direction as all do what they think is right.
• Encourages loyalty as it gives responsibility to the employee.	• Poor coordination can lead to inefficiency.
• Employees can use all their skills for the benefit of the business.	• This style can lead to conflicts between team members.

Table 7.06 Advantages and disadvantages of laissez-faire management.

TERMS

Autocratic leadership style: managers make all the decisions without any discussion with employees.

Democratic leadership style: managers make decisions after consultation with employees.

Laissez-faire leadership style: managers leave employees to make day-to-day decisions.

Factors to consider when deciding which leadership style to use:

- **Manager's own characteristics** – is the manager naturally autocratic or democratic?

- **Characteristics of the group** – do employees respond better to instructions, or being able to decide what to do on their own?

- **The task** – is it straightforward or complex?

- **Type of business** – creative businesses will have a different approach from a factory making standard products.

7.07 The role of trade unions

Unions represent individual employees to stop employers trying to exploit them. They use collective bargaining: a union represents all members as a group in negotiations. This gives the union more influence to help members get a better deal.

TERM

Trade union: a group of employees who join together to protect the interests of its members.

Sample question

TCS is a large steel manufacturer. The Managing Director has announced plans to make 1000 of its 3500 employees redundant. She said: 'Labour and energy costs are too high. TCS cannot compete against cheap imports. In other countries, employees do long hours for minimum wages.' All TCS employees are members of a trade union.

Explain **two** effects on TCS's employees of being members of a trade union. **[8]**

Sample answer:
Effect 1: Strength in numbers. TCS is more likely to listen to 3500 employees rather than individuals, so a union could get the best deal possible for the 1000 employees at risk of redundancy. **[4]**

Effect 2: Improved working conditions. A union negotiates to ensure that the factory is a safe place to work so that employees do not become overtired from working long hours. **[4]**

TIP

Do not use the same explanation for each point. This is repetition, and will not improve the quality of your answer.

Benefits	Drawbacks
• Negotiate with employers for better pay. This could increase the living standards for its members. • Provide additional services and social facilities. • Provide legal advice and support. • Negotiate with employers for better working conditions. • Represent employees in cases of discrimination and unfair dismissal.	• Employees have to pay membership fees to the union. • Individual members are bound by the decisions of the majority, even if they don't agree with them. • Employees will lose wages during any strike action. • Individual employees cannot negotiate for themselves with the employer. • Unions can fine or take action against members who break union rules.

Table 7.07 Benefits and drawbacks for employees of being union members.

Benefits	Drawbacks
• Unions provide a single point of contact between employers and employees for negotiations – simpler and less time consuming than having to negotiate with each individual employee. • Unions help to improve working conditions and health and safety in the workplace. This can improve employee motivation and reduce absenteeism or labour turnover.	• Powerful unions can often force employers to meet high wage demands. This increases business costs and could reduce the competitiveness and profitability of the business. • Unions could use industrial action, such as strikes, to try and force employers to meet their demands. This can disrupt production and result in loss of orders, which reduces profitability.

Table 7.08 Benefits and drawbacks for employers of employees being union members.

Progress check

1 Name **one** purpose of an organisational chart.

2 Identify **two** factors that affect the span of control.

3 Name **three** main different ways in which a business can be organised.

4 Explain **one** benefit of a decentralised structure.

Summary

There are a number of technical terms to learn that relate to simple organisational charts. Try to understand the relationship between the various concepts. Managers have many roles to carry out and will use different approaches to leadership. Each leadership style has its advantages and disadvantages, so not all are appropriate for any situation. Trade unions can offer a number of benefits to employees.

Sample questions

Splash Active (SA) specialises in providing activity holidays for families. SA prides itself on its good reputation and competitive prices. SA has won awards for its good customer service and health and safety. SA's organisational structure has a wide span of control and a short chain of command. Employees are seen as an important factor in its success. Few employees leave. All employees are paid by time rate. All managers have a democratic leadership style. Most managers think that praise is the best way to motivate employees.

Example 1:
Identify **two** functions of management. [2]

Sample answer:
Function 1: Coordination. [1]
Function 2: Planning. [1]

Example 2:
Outline **two** advantages to SA of having a wide span of control. [4]

Sample answer:
Advantage 1: A wide span encourages delegation [1], and helps employees believe that they are important [1].

Advantage 2: It improves communication [1], helping SA offer good customer service [1].

Example 3:
Explain **two** advantages to SA of having a democratic leadership style. [6]

Sample answer:
Advantage 1: There is better quality service [1] as otherwise it would be difficult for managers to oversee all employees [1]; this helps to build the business's good reputation [1].

Advantage 2: It helps to motivate employees [1] as they feel part of decision-making [1], and as a result, few employees leave [1].

Examination-style questions

Wooden Works (WW) makes hand-finished furniture, which it sells nationally in country T. To cope with growing demand, the management wants to reorganise the business by region rather than by function. The leadership style at WW is autocratic, but there are plans to encourage managers to change this. 'Who needs delegation? Employees work. They do not need to know about planning or which tables to make,' said the Operations manager. WW does not allow employees to join trade unions.

a   Define 'trade union'.   [2]

b   Outline **two** advantages to WW of organising the business by region.

Advantage 1:
Advantage 2:   [4]

c   Explain **one** advantage and **one** disadvantage to WW of using delegation.
Advantage:
Disadvantage: [6]

d   State the advantages and disadvantages of the following **three** leadership styles WW could use. Which style do you think WW should use? Justify your answer.
Autocratic:
Democratic:
Laissez-faire:
Conclusion: [12]

8.01 Recruitment and selection

All businesses need to find new employees when the business expands or employees leave. Recruitment is all about finding and selecting the right person for a particular job.

8.02 Difference between internal and external recruitment

Internal recruitment tries to recruit a new person from current employees. Methods include newsletters, notice boards, emails and word of mouth from other employees (this means what other employees say).

External recruitment looks to attract applicants from outside the business.

Methods include:

- **Local newspapers** – mainly used for unskilled jobs.

- **National newspapers** – used for senior positions, or where few skilled employees are available locally.

- **Specialist magazines** – useful for technical/skilled jobs.

- **Recruitment agencies** – often used if the business has little experience in recruiting. Also helpful if the business wants to hide activities from competitors.

- **Job websites or business website** – can attract people from anywhere in the world, or those interested in a particular business.

- **Government-run centres** – provide services to employers and employees to help match employees to jobs. This helps the government to reduce unemployment levels.

The choice of method depends on the job involved, the time and money available for recruitment as well as economic factors such as employment levels.

	Internal recruitment	External recruitment
Cost issues	• Likely to be quicker and cheaper. • The business will have another person's job to replace.	• Likely to be more expensive to recruit. • Induction training also needed.
Familiarisation	• Employees already know how business operates.	• Takes time to learn how the business works.
Choice of candidates	• Limited choice. • Existing employees might not have right skills.	• Wider choice. • Helps bring new ideas, skills and experience to business.
Impact on other employees	• Depends. Can motivate or lead to jealousy between employees.	• Can cause resentment if internal candidate feels overlooked.

Table 8.01 Differences between internal and external recruitment.

8.03 The main stages in the recruitment and selection process

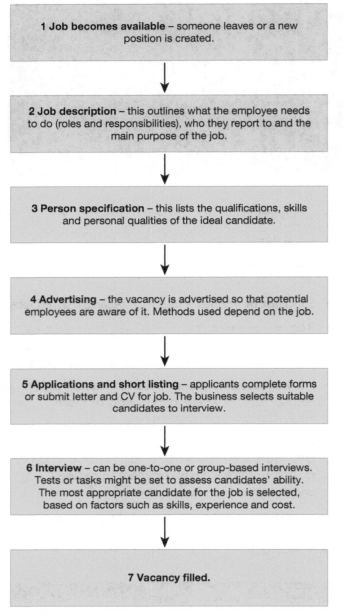

1 Job becomes available – someone leaves or a new position is created.

2 Job description – this outlines what the employee needs to do (roles and responsibilities), who they report to and the main purpose of the job.

3 Person specification – this lists the qualifications, skills and personal qualities of the ideal candidate.

4 Advertising – the vacancy is advertised so that potential employees are aware of it. Methods used depend on the job.

5 Applications and short listing – applicants complete forms or submit letter and CV for job. The business selects suitable candidates to interview.

6 Interview – can be one-to-one or group-based interviews. Tests or tasks might be set to assess candidates' ability. The most appropriate candidate for the job is selected, based on factors such as skills, experience and cost.

7 Vacancy filled.

Figure 8.01 The main stages in the recruitment and selection process.

TERMS

Job description: a written description of what the job involves.

Person specification: this describes the type of person needed for the job.

8.04 Benefits and limitations of part-time and full-time employees

Most employees have a contract which sets out the number of hours they will usually work. Full-time employees will have a higher number of set hours compared to part-time employees.

	Part-time work	Full-time work
Benefits	• Flexible – can help at busy times • Keep experienced employees as they can fit work around other commitments • More cost-effective as the business need only pay when the work is required	• More committed to business • Likely to be better trained • Better quality service possible • Fewer people to train
Limitations	• Additional recruitment costs • Communication issues • Not as easy to coordinate operations • Are they committed to business?	• More expensive labour costs • Less flexible

Table 8.02 Benefits and limitations of part-time and full-time work.

TIP

There is no set number of hours for full- and part-time employees. This will vary between countries and industries.

8.05 The different methods of training

Training is important as it:

- increases employees' skills in their current job to increase productivity
- develops skills for future jobs
- motivates employees so they feel valued
- makes business more flexible if employees can do more than one job
- reduces mistakes to help improve profitability.

There are three main types of training – induction, on-the-job and off-the-job.

Induction training

- This might include health and safety information or a tour of the building.
- It provides an opportunity to communicate culture.
- People know who to ask if there is a problem.
- It can help new employees to settle quickly into the work environment.
- It can prevent costly mistakes as employees know what to do.
- There can be increased business costs.
- It can cause a delay to when people can start to work.

Differences between on-the-job and off-the-job training

	On-the-job	Off-the-job
What it is	Employees learn job-specific skills while working	Employees learn skills away from the actual work location
Where it happens	At workplace	Away from workplace
Way of learning	By doing real work	Gain knowledge or practise
Trained by	Experienced employees	Experts and specialists
Relative cost	Inexpensive	Expensive
Output during training	Some – but slows down trainer as well	None – but other employees not disrupted
Quality issues	Mistakes can damage quality and image	Higher quality of training possible

Table 8.03 Differences between on-the-job and off-the-job training.

TIP

Training is not free. It will cost time, money and even output as employees are learning new skills.

TERMS

Induction training: this type of training introduces new people to the business, familiarising them with the business procedures and meeting other employees.

Off-the-job training: employees learn the skills needed for a job in a different location to the actual work place

On-the-job training: employees learn job-specific skills while they are working.

8.06 The difference between dismissal and redundancy

Redundancy occurs when the employer has to release employees to reduce costs, or the job they did is no longer needed.

- The employee has not done anything wrong.
- The employee is often entitled to some compensation.

Dismissal happens when the employee is told to leave as they have broken the terms of their contract.

TERMS

Dismissal: the employment contract ends due to unreasonable behaviour or poor performance by the employee.

Redundancy: the employee is released because the job they did is no longer needed.

8.07 Downsizing the workforce

There are times when a business will need to reduce the number of employees. In such situations a business needs to decide who to make redundant.

> **Reasons to downsize:**
> - Automation
> - Closure of site
> - Relocation
> - Merger
> - Changes in market demand
> - Reduce costs

Figure 8.02 Situations when downsizing the workforce might be necessary.

Sample question

TCS is a steel manufacturer. The Managing Director has announced plans to make 1000 of its 3500 employees redundant. She said: 'Labour and energy costs are too high. TCS cannot compete against cheap imports. In other countries employees do long hours for minimum wages.' All TCS employees are members of a trade union.

With reference to TCS, outline the difference between redundancy and dismissal. **[4]**

Sample answer:

Redundancy means that the job no longer exists. Because of cheap imports, TCS does not need to make as much steel, so does not need to employ as many employees. If the employees lost their jobs because they had done something wrong, that would be dismissal.

> **Factors to consider**
> - Identify which jobs are not essential
> - Performance/experience/skills
> - Wages/salary
> - Length of service/cost of redundancy
> - Attitude/attendance/disciplinary record
> - Other issues, for example, close to retirement

Figure 8.03 Factors to consider when downsizing a workforce.

8.08 Legal controls over employment

A successful business needs to have a good relationship between employers and employees. It is a balancing act as each group wants different things.

Laws exist to ensure fair treatment of employees. Businesses cannot avoid laws. They could face legal action, which would increase business costs.

Areas covered by the law include the following:

- **Minimum wage laws** – guarantees all employees a basic amount for each hour worked or output produced.

- **Employment contract** – states the terms of the job and what to do if there are any problems. This can be used to help resolve disagreements.

- **Protection against discrimination** – ensures that employees are not unfairly treated because of their gender, race or any physical disabilities.

- **Health and Safety laws** – these set minimum standards for safe working conditions.

Figure 8.04 Balancing the wants of employers and employees.

Example of health and safety law	How law might affect business
Maximum hours of work	• Might need to recruit more employees to ensure that production is finished • Offers overtime payments • Introduces breaks
Protection from dangerous machinery	• Adding guards to equipment or providing extra training
Provision of safety equipment and clothing	• Providing harnesses, goggles, safety helmets or clothing
Lighting and heating	• Installing extra heaters or fans, or extra lighting into building
Basic hygiene facilities	• Installing extra toilets or washing facilities

Table 8.04 How health and safety law affects business.

Laws may not always help employees:

- Many businesses already pay above minimum wages.

- To reduce costs, a business might relocate to another country or change its production methods. Jobs might be at risk.

- Employees' hours could be restricted. This limits the amount they can earn.

TIP

Every country has different laws. You do not need to learn specific examples but be aware of the issues covered by the law.

Summary

The recruitment process involves a number of stages. Each stage has an important role to play when selecting the right candidate for a job. Training can take many forms. There will be times when a business has to reduce the size of its workforce. Legal controls exist to ensure employers do not unfairly treat employees.

Progress check

1 Outline the main stages in the recruitment process.

2 When is induction training used?

3 State **one** difference between off-the-job and on-the-job training.

4 What is the purpose of legal controls over employment?

Sample questions

Snapper makes shoes. Due to falling sales, the Finance Director plans to downsize. The business will close its factory in either country A or B. All employees are given off-the-job training.

	Factory A	Factory B
Output per week (pairs of shoes)	145 000	120 000
Number of employees	1 000	800
Labour cost per hour	$3.50	$4.00
Average hourly wage in country	$2.75	$3.95
Union membership	5 000	3 000

Table 8.05 Comparison information on factory A and factory B.

Example 1:

Identify **two** reasons (other than falling sales) why a business might downsize. [2]

Sample answer:
Reason 1: Automation. [1]

Reason 2: Economic recession. [1]

Example 2:

Explain **two** benefits to Snapper of using off-the-job training. [6]

Sample answer:
Benefit 1: This will not distract other employees [1] so they are able to focus on making shoes [1] and keep output high [1].

Benefit 2: Employees can learn new skills **[1]** such as new fabrics and stitching **[1]**, so they are able to make more or different products **[1]**.

Example 3:

Explain **two** factors Snapper would need to consider when deciding which employees to make redundant. **[8]**

Sample answer:

Factor 1: Experience **[1]**: the business will want to get rid of employees who make mistakes **[1]** as faulty shoes need to be remade **[1]** which will lower the level of factory output **[1]**.

Factor 2: Identify non-essential jobs **[1]**: it might be difficult for someone to cut leather **[1]** whereas many people could do polishing **[1]**, so it would cost too much to recruit these people if they are needed in future **[1]**.

Examination-style questions

Stay@ is a luxury hotel. It has 45 rooms and is located near six other hotels. Stay@ has 20 full-time and 40 part-time employees who all receive on-the-job training. Demand is seasonal. When busy, employees all work long hours. The hotel plans to increase its income by expanding the fitness centre at the hotel. The Human Resources manager needs to recruit two skilled fitness trainers. She knows there are many legal controls over employment issues to be considered.

a   Define 'on-the-job training'. [2]

b   Outline **two** areas of legal controls over employment that Stay@ needs to consider.
Area 1:
Area 2: [4]

c   Explain **two** advantages to Stay@ of using part-time employees.
Advantage 1:
Advantage 2: [6]

d   Explain why each of the following stages of the recruitment and selection process are important to Stay@ when choosing suitable employees. Justify your answer.
Job description:
Person specification:
Advertisement: [12]

9.01 The importance of effective communication

Communication is simply a method of sending a message from one person (sender) to another person or group (receiver).

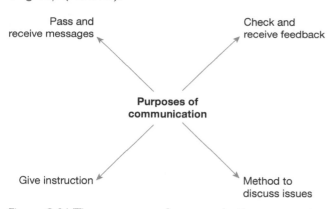

Figure 9.01 The purposes of communication.

Effective communication means that the correct message has been sent using an appropriate method, received and understood.

This is important, for many reasons:

• The right products are made or jobs done, so less time and resources are wasted.

• Correct decisions are taken. Wrong decisions can lead to inefficiency and lower profitability.

• Motivation improves. Employees feel valued, so less likely to leave.

• Maintaining business image: customer dissatisfaction could mean fewer sales.

• Better coordination: for example, suppliers want to know when materials are needed. Lenders want to be kept informed about financial requirements.

9.02 The difference between internal and external communication

Communication happens between people both inside and outside the business organisation.

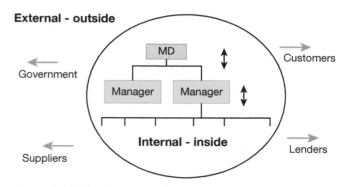

Figure 9.02 The features of internal and external communication.

TIP

Internal communication can be at a single site or between the business's various locations around the world.

9.03 Methods of communication

Communication can be either one-way or two-way.

One-way: person receiving message cannot reply to it.	**Two-way:** person receiving message can give feedback.
Sender → Receiver	Sender ←→ Receiver
• A manager gives instruction but employees cannot confirm that they have understood the message.	• Both sender and receiver are involved in communication.
• Mistakes are possible as there is no feedback.	• Feedback allows both to check that the message has been received and understood.
Examples: memos, notice boards, posters.	Examples: meetings, telephone, video conferencing.

Table 9.01 The difference between one-way and two-way communication.

There are three main categories of communication:

- verbal
- written communication
- visual.

Each method has different uses. Most methods can be used for both internal and external communication.

Verbal

Examples: one-to-one conversations, group meetings, telephone calls and video conferencing.

Advantages	Disadvantages
• Information can be quickly sent	• No permanent record
• Understanding/feedback is easy to obtain as there is direct contact	• In large meetings, you cannot tell if everyone is listening or has understood the message
• Can use body language/ gestures to support message	• Care is needed with telephone as one cannot see the other person
• Allows same message to be given to many people at same time	• Both sender and receiver need good communication skills
• Able to gain instant response	• Face-to-face meetings are not always possible

Table 9.02 Advantages and disadvantages of verbal methods.

Written communication

Examples: letters, emails, text messages, faxes, reports, websites and social media.

Advantages	Disadvantages
• Permanent record of communication can be kept	• Direct feedback is not always possible
• Useful if a lot of detail needs to be sent	• Language might be difficult for some to understand
• Message can be copied for many people to read	• Cannot always check if message has been received
• Emails/text allow for quick and cheap messages to be sent	• Some forms of written communication can be ignored or seen too late

Table 9.03 Advantages and disadvantages of written communication methods.

Visual

Examples: posters, charts, PowerPoint presentations and videos.

Advantages	Disadvantages
• Diagrams help people to understand technical information	• No feedback
• Information is summarised, so message is received quickly	• People can interpret information in different ways
• Can use pictures to show emotions	• Can be difficult to show some information in visual form

Table 9.04 Advantages and disadvantages of visual methods.

> **TIP**
> Verbal, written and visual are categories not methods of communication. If you are asked to identify a method, name a specific example.

> **TIP**
> Methods are useful for different purposes. Choosing the right method to use in a given situation is vital for effective communication.

9.04 Factors to consider when choosing a method of communication

- **What is the message** – how much information needs to be sent?
- **Why is it being sent** – is it confidential information, or general information for all to see?
- **Who needs to know** – how many people is the message being sent to?
- **How quickly does it need to reach them** – urgent messages need a quick method, but this is likely to be more expensive to send.
- **Is written evidence needed?**

> **TIP**
>
> Organisational structure can impact on communication. A tall hierarchy might mean messages are received too slowly.

Technology now plays an important role in communication. It offers many benefits such as speed (email, text), sending detailed information via websites and email attachments for both internal and external purposes. Do not forget the drawbacks though – cost, security concerns and reliability issues.

> **TERMS**
>
> Communication: a method of sending a message from one person (sender) to another person/group (receiver).
>
> External communication: communication that takes place with people outside the organisation.
>
> Internal communication: communication that takes place between people within the same organisation.

Sample question

Amber owns a small fabric business. As fashion is always changing, Amber knows it is important to communicate with her customers.

Explain **two** methods of communication Amber might use. [6]

> **Sample answer:**
> **Method 1:** Email, as Amber can include pictures of sample fabrics so her customers can see what the choices are. [3]
>
> **Method 2:** Phone, so Amber can call to notify customers straightaway when the new designs are available. [3]

9.05 Barriers to effective communication and ways to overcome them

Communication has four elements: see Figure 9.03.

For communication to be effective, the receiver has to receive and understand the message sent. If any part of the process breaks down, this **barrier** will stop the message from getting through as intended.

Problems can arise at any stage of the communication process.

→ The sender – wrong message sent, speaking too quickly.

→ The message itself – too much information, inappropriate language used.

→ The method of communication used – technical problems.

→ The receiver – not listening or receives unclear message.

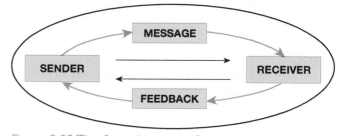

Figure 9.03 The four elements of communication.

> **TERM**
>
> Barriers to communication: any factor which causes a breakdown in communication.

Sample question

VNJ makes customised motorbikes. It imports parts from suppliers and sells the finished bikes in many countries. The Operations Director is worried about barriers to communication. She said, 'I don't understand why the inventory is so low. Customer complaints have increased.'

Outline **two** possible barriers to communication for VNJ. **[4]**

Sample answer:

Barrier 1: Language – customers from different countries cannot clearly explain the features they want on the bikes. **[2]**

Barrier 2: Problem with messages – inventory orders from suppliers are not received on time. **[2]**

Barriers and possible solutions

Barrier	Problem	Method to overcome it
Language	Receiver does not understand the message	• Keep language simple and message short. • Avoid technical terms. • Be aware of translation errors if message is sent overseas.
Noise	Background sounds so message is not heard clearly	• Choose suitable method to communicate, for example, written. • Keep message simple; ask for feedback.
Timing	Wrong channel used so message is not received on time	• Choose method that allows for quick response, for example, text, phone.
Technical breakdown	Message not received due to faulty equipment	• Check that method used is reliable; ask for feedback.
Atmosphere	Message not understood as sender and receiver do not trust each other	• Ask for feedback. • Choose a method where they can see each other, for example, videoconference, meeting.

Barrier	Problem	Method to overcome it
Sender does not receive response	Sender unaware of receiver's decision	• Ask for feedback to check that the message is understood.
Receiver not listening	Receiver might not be paying attention	• Keep message simple and clear. • Ask for feedback.

Table 9.05 Overcoming barriers to communications.

TIP

If you are asked to identify **barriers to communication**, remember to look at the context. Suggestions need to be suitable for the size and type of business in question.

Progress check

1 State **two** purposes of communication.

2 Identify **two** advantages of verbal communication.

3 State **two** factors to consider when choosing a method of communication.

4 Explain the difference between one-way and two-way communication.

Summary

Communication is important. A business will use a number of different types of communication to convey messages effectively. For each situation, different methods will be useful, so being able to choose and justify an appropriate method is essential. Poor communication can cause problems, but there are many possible ways to overcome the barriers to communication.

Sample questions

FCB is a successful insurance business. It has 50 branches with 800 employees across country P. The Managing Director wants to improve internal communication by introducing new technology into its branches. He says, 'Customers complain about slow service. Memos never reach me, documents are everywhere and many part-time employees complain they don't know what is happening.'

Example 1:
Define 'internal communication'. **[2]**

Sample answer:
This is communication that takes place between people in the organisation. **[2]**

Example 2:
Explain **two** possible reasons why FCB might want to improve communication. **[6]**

Sample answer:
Reason 1: Lower cost **[1]** as paper is needed for writing out policies **[1]** that couldn't easily be found **[1]**.

Reason 2: Offer better service **[1]** so the business receives fewer complaints **[1]** and attracts/keeps customers **[1]**.

Example 3:
Explain **two** ways in which new technology can help improve communication at FCB. **[8]**

Sample answer:
Way 1: Emails can be sent quickly and easily **[1]** to all 800 employees at same time **[1]**; there is more chance that everyone is kept up to date **[1]**; this can help FCB provide a better service **[1]**.

Way 2: Better security **[1]** as sensitive insurance documents can safely be stored online **[1]**, rather than in one of the 50 branches **[1]**, where they could be found by other customers/others and risk damaging FCB's reputation **[1]**.

Examination-style questions

BLW make carpets using batch production. It sells its products to a number of large shops across the country. In order to reduce costs, BLW wants to introduce a new inventory control system into its factory. BLW needs to tell its four suppliers about the change. The Operations Director knows effective communication will be important. He said, 'We cannot have any barriers to communication.'

a   Define 'barrier to communication'.   [2]

b   Explain **two** reasons why effective communication might be important for BLW.
Reason 1:
Reason 2:   [6]

c   Explain **two** methods of communication BLW might use to communicate with its customers.
Method 1:
Method 2:   [8]

d   Consider the advantages and disadvantages of the following **three** methods of communication BLW could use to inform suppliers about the change. Which method do you think BLW should use? Justify your answer.
Meeting:
Email:
Telephone:
Recommendation: [12]

TIP
Feedback is important, so two-way methods of communication are often better.

Section 3:
MARKETING

Marketing, competition and the customer

Learning summary

By the end of this unit you should understand:

- [ ] the role of marketing in identifying and satisfying customer needs

- [ ] market changes, and how a business might respond

- [ ] ways to maintain customer loyalty and build customer relationships

- [ ] concepts of niche marketing and mass marketing

- [ ] how and why market segmentation is undertaken.

10.01 Role of marketing

Marketing is more than just advertising and promotion. It involves:

- **Identifying** – finding out what customers want. Market research is key (see 11.01).

- **Anticipating** – what customers might demand changes all the time. Looking ahead to spot the 'next big thing' is important so that the business is able to respond quickly.

- **Satisfying** – providing products where, when and at a price customers will pay.

- **Profit** – profit is needed so that the business can afford to invest in areas such as production and research.

TERMS

Cost-effective: when the financial return is worth the expenditure.

Marketing: anticipating, identifying and satisfying customer needs – at a profit.

10.02 Building customer relationships and maintaining customer loyalty

Retaining existing customers is more cost-effective than attracting new ones.

Current customers know your product, and if they like it, they might buy again. They can also tell friends and family, which is free promotion.

Ways to build customer relationships and maintain loyalty

- Offer good/personal service, for example, be friendly with customers.

- Find out what customers want, and offer the right product.

- Ask for feedback.

- Offer extra services, for example, delivery, credit terms, after sales, longer opening hours.

- Resolve complaints quickly/offer refunds.

- Communicate with customers regularly, for example, newsletters or mailshots.

- Reward customer loyalty, for example, loyalty cards, special offers.

- Train employees so that they can provide a better service.

10.03 Why consumer spending patterns may change

Customer needs change. People spend their money on different things at different times. This is affected by the following factors:

- **Price** – normally, the higher the price, the lower the demand.

- **Income** – a change in income will alter what people can afford to buy.

- **Taste/fashion** – what people like can change over time.

- **Price of alternative goods** – if similar products are cheaper to buy, demand for the original item might fall.

- **Price of complementary goods** – the sales of some products depend on the price of other items.

- **Population** – the age, gender and size of population can influence what and how much is demanded.

- **Seasonal factors** – demand can vary with the time of year.

- **Government policy and laws** – laws can restrict/stop production and the purchase of certain goods; fiscal and monetary policies influence confidence and the amount of money people have to spend.

- **Technological changes** – this makes new products possible.

Businesses also try to influence spending patterns through product, pricing and promotion decisions.

It is important to be aware of changing customer needs. Businesses must react to changes to remain competitive. Any change will affect many business decisions – production levels, advertising and inventory. Customers have power. They will switch to a rival business if their needs and wants are not satisfied. Sales will be lost.

10.04 Why some markets have become more competitive

Often there are many businesses trying to sell to the same customers. Why?

- **Rising living standards** – people have more income available to spend.

- **Globalisation** – more choice as products and suppliers available internationally.

- **Technology/internet** – new production technology and the rise of e-commerce.

- **Government policies** – these can encourage competition.

10.05 How businesses can respond to market changes and competition

Businesses must remain competitive to survive. How can a business do this?

- **Know your customers** – so that you can provide what they want.

- **Differentiate** – so that customers do not want to choose a competitor.

- **Look for new markets** – to increase the range of customers and spread risk.

- **Keep up to date** – review current products, invest in new technology, find new materials or suppliers.

- **Manage costs** – so the business is able to keep prices affordable.

- **Develop new products** – to keep up to date.

- **Maintain customers' loyalty** – to keep market share.

All this takes time and money, and there is no guarantee of success.

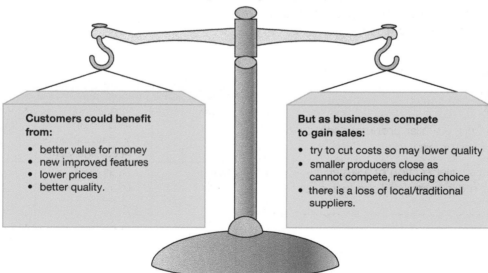

Is increased competition good for customers?

Customers could benefit from:
- better value for money
- new improved features
- lower prices
- better quality.

But as businesses compete to gain sales:
- try to cut costs so may lower quality
- smaller producers close as cannot compete, reducing choice
- there is a loss of local/traditional suppliers.

Figure 10.01 Advantages and disadvantages for customers of increased competition.

Sample question

CDY makes sports equipment. The Marketing Director has been looking at some data. Product A, a tennis racket, has been its best-selling product for many years.

Explain **two** possible reasons for the change in market share for product A shown in Figure 10.02. **[6]**

Sample answer:

Reason 1: Change in technology. As the product has been selling for many years, it has become outdated, so customers are looking for newer rackets. **[3]**

Reason 2: New competitors. Consumers have different sports companies to choose from, reducing the demand for CDY's products. **[3]**

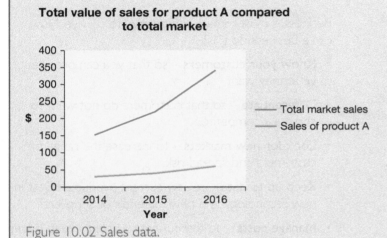

Figure 10.02 Sales data.

10.06 Niche marketing and mass marketing

A market is the place where buyers and sellers are brought together. A target market is the specific group or segment of customers that the product is directed at. Most markets can be divided into either a mass market or niche market.

Figure 10.03 The difference between a niche market and mass market.

TERMS

Mass market: where a similar product is sold to a large number of customers.

Niche market: a smaller section of a larger market, where a more specialised product is sold.

	Niche	Mass
Target market	• Specialised, focused on specific customer needs and wants	• Wide – can sell to most people
Size of market	• Small with limited potential for growth	• Large, so higher sales and profit potential
	• Less competition as market size deters larger businesses	• Competitive market, so difficult to dominate market

	Niche	Mass
Prices	• May be able to charge more if customers pay extra for specialism • Higher profit margin possible	• Lower as there are many competitors • Low profit margin likely
Scale of production	• Small, so harder to decrease unit costs	• Large, so economies of scale possible
Risk	• High risk if demand falls as it is a specialist market	• Risk spread as likely to sell a number of products
Threats	• Success can attract larger competitors	• Many customers want something different from mass market products

Table 10.01 Differences between niche marketing and mass marketing.

10.07 Market segmentation

Dividing up the market into particular groups (segments) of people allows a business to better match their products to their customer's needs.

Age, gender, income, interests, location, socio-economic group and size of households can be used to segment markets.

Segmentation can help businesses to:

• develop new and existing products to better match customer requirements – increase sales and profits

• spot gaps in the market – opportunities to increase customer base

• promote goods more effectively – as the business can reach target customers more easily.

TERM

Segmentation: dividing up the market into particular groups of people.

Sample question

PGN is a book publishing business.

Outline **two** ways PGN could segment the market. **[4]**

Sample answer:
Way 1: Age. Children want picture books, while adults will be happy with words. **[2]**

Way 2: Interests. Some people like food and others want to read about sport. **[2]**

Summary

Demand can change, and this can influence business actions. Increasing competition affects both consumers and businesses. There are two main types of market – niche and mass. Focusing on either has implications for production, finance and risk. Segmentation helps a business to target its products at the right customers.

Progress check

1 Identify **two** reasons for marketing.
2 State **two** features of a niche market.
3 Explain **one** benefit of segmentation to business
4 Outline **one** possible disadvantage for customers of increased competition.

Sample questions

Bradbury makes luxury handmade chocolates aimed at high-income customers. It is a niche market. Last year sales increased by 20%. The Marketing manager said, 'I wasn't expecting demand to change that much.' She knows that maintaining customer loyalty is important, but cannot decide whether offering discounts or sending newsletters is the best method to use.

Example 1:
Define 'niche market'. **[2]**

Sample answer:
A niche market is a smaller section of the larger market **[1]**, which usually sells specialised products **[1]**.

Example 2:
Explain **two** factors that might affect demand for Bradbury's products. **[6]**

Sample answer:
Factor 1: Income **[1]** as it is a luxury product **[1]**; people are likely to buy more if incomes rise, as they have more money to spend **[1]**.

Factor 2: Tastes **[1]**: people will want to try different flavours **[1]** as they try to keep up with fashion. **[1]**.

Example 3:
Do you think offering discounts or sending newsletters is the best way for Bradbury to maintain customer loyalty? Justify your answer. **[6]**

Sample answer:
Newsletters can keep people up to date **[1]** with any new chocolates **[1]** so customers may be interested to try **[1]**. Discounts would lower the price, which can encourage more customers to buy the product **[1]**.

I would not use discounts as this would cost money and could damage the reputation of the business **[1]** and lower rather than maintain sales, so I would recommend a newsletter as it helps people remember what the business has to offer **[1]**.

Examination-style questions

Dwayne is a qualified teacher. He wants to set up a home-tutoring business. He has carried out some market research so knows there is demand. His target market is 14–16-year-old IGCSE students. Marketing will be very important to his business. He knows he will have to build customer relationships if he is to be successful.

a Define 'target market'. [2]

b Explain **two** benefits to Dwayne of building good customer relationships.
Benefit 1:
Benefit 2: [6]

c Explain **two** possible reasons why marketing will be important to Dwayne's business.
Reason 1:
Reason 2: [8]

d Explain how the following **three** ways could help Dwayne build good customer relationships. Which way do you think will be the most effective for Dwayne to use? Justify your answer.
Loyalty schemes:
Ask for feedback:
Train employees:
Recommendation: [12]

TIP When you make a decision, justify it, and explain why you have not picked the other options.

Market research

Learning summary

By the end of this chapter you should understand:

- [ ] the uses of market research information

- [ ] the methods of primary and secondary research, and limitations of each

- [ ] factors affecting the accuracy of market research data

- [ ] how market research results are presented and used.

11.01 Uses of market research information

Market-orientated businesses take customer needs into account before developing the product. This ensures that the products made are what customers are willing to buy. Knowing customers' needs can help a business to remain competitive as well as maintain loyalty and sales.

Accurate market research helps provide information:

- about market and competitors

- to identify the needs of current and potential customers

- to help reduce the risk of launching new or improved products

- to help plan marketing campaigns

- to help solve business problems, such as falling sales.

Information gathered can be either **quantitative** or **qualitative**.

Quantitative

Quantitative information is numerical: it does not provide the reasons behind the information, but it is easy to present as a graph or chart.

Examples: questionnaires and surveys.

Qualitative

Qualitative information is factual, based on opinions and reasons. It can provide detailed information, but is difficult to present in charts as it is hard to compare opinions.

Examples: interviews and focus groups

TERMS

Market research: process of collecting and analysing information about customers or a market.

Market-orientated: this describes a business which takes customer needs into account before developing a product.

The different methods of collecting information are classified as either **primary** or **secondary** market research.

11.02 Differences between primary and secondary market research

	Primary	Secondary
Meaning	Involves collecting new information that did not exist before	Involves using information that already exists
Alternative name	Field research	Desk research
Type of information	New	Existing
Cost	Relatively expensive	Relatively cheap as information either free or available for a small fee
Time taken to collect	Time-consuming as new information	Quick/easy to access as it is already available
Access to results	Only available to business	Anyone can see it, including competitors

	Primary	**Secondary**
Focus of research	Specific to individual requirements	May not be relevant for current purposes
Relevance	High as collected for specific purpose	Can be out of date
Useful for	Specific issues, for example, product changes	General information, for example, population
Other points to consider	Not always feasible, as might not be able to access target customers	Could include additional helpful information not previously considered

Table 11.01 Primary and secondary market research.

TERMS

Primary market research: involves collecting new information for a specific purpose.

Secondary market research: involves using information that already exists and was collected for another purpose.

TIP

Choice of method depends on time available, cost and what the business wants to know.

11.03 Methods of primary market research

- **Postal questionnaires or online surveys** – uses a list of set questions.
  - ✓ easier to compare results
  - ✗ risk of bias
  - ✗ can take a long time to collect.
- **Interviews** – similar to questionnaire; uses open questions and fewer people asked.
  - ✓ allows for detailed information
  - ✗ risk of bias.

- **Observation** – watching or recording what people do or buy.
  - ✓ relatively cheap
  - ✗ provides basic information.
- **Consumer panels/focus groups** – a selection of people who have similar characteristics to target market who give their opinions on a product/service.
  - ✓ detailed information
  - ✗ expensive and time-consuming to arrange.

11.04 Methods of secondary market research

- **Own sales information** – records of previous years' sales.
- **Government statistics** – information about population, income, economic data.
- **Newspaper/internet articles** – general information on markets or trading conditions/trends in the market.
- **Trade organisations** – industry-specific data for its members.
- **Market research agencies** – these agencies carry out research for other people. Results are available for a fee.

TIP

The main difference between primary and secondary research is the type of information gained.

11.05 The need for sampling

It would take too much money and time to ask everyone for their views and opinions. Businesses can only ask a small number of the population (sample). The business tries to create a sample which will represent the views of all potential customers. A larger sample size should reduce the chance of bias.

Sample question

Dwayne is a qualified teacher. He wants to set up a home tutoring business. He has carried out some market research. His target market is 14–16-year-old IGCSE students. Dwayne knows he will have to build customer relationships if he is to be successful. He is not sure how legal controls will affect any marketing decisions.

Explain **two** methods of market research Dwayne might have used. **[8]**

Sample answer:
Method 1: A questionnaire is a suitable research method for Dwayne. He could create a questionnaire to ask a sample of people a set of questions, to find out whether they are interested in having tutoring, which subjects they require and what sort of help they are looking for. **[4]**

Method 2: Government statistics will give Dwayne information about the population. He will be able to see how many 14–16-year-olds are in the area, and the type and quality of schools available to see how big his target market is likely to be. **[4]**

TIP

Unless the question states otherwise, you can discuss any appropriate methods.

TERM

Sampling: research based on a small number of the population.

11.06 Factors affecting accuracy of market research data

Any market research can produce information that is unreliable or inaccurate. Biased information can lead to the wrong decisions being made, which could result in higher costs, wasted resources and lost revenue. Factors include:

- **Cost and time** – the more accurate and relevant the research, the longer and more expensive it will be

to collect. Does the business have enough time to collect 'perfect' data?

- **Methodology** – is there any bias? Does it contain poorly worded, leading or wrong questions? How large is the sample? Who is being asked? Will people just say what they think the researcher wants to hear?

- **People's views change over time** – what the customers were happy to buy in the past could be different now. Income, tastes and other factors can affect their opinions.

- **Is it a new product?** – do customers understand what the product is?

11.07 Presentation of market research data

It is important to display the information in a form that is easy to understand. The method chosen depends on what information needs to be presented and whom it is for.

Tables

These are a simple record of facts and figures presented in rows and columns. They are useful to show a lot of detailed information but it is not easy to see trends quickly.

Worked example

Cool Clothing

Cool Clothing (CC) sells their products all over the world. The Marketing Director plans to expand the number of outlets but cannot decide where to open them. Table 11.02 shows the market research results.

Country	Value of sales ($m)
A	8
B	5
C	18
D	6
V	12
W	7

Table 11.02 The value of CC's sales in each country.

What does this show?

Country C has the highest sales of $18m, followed by country V with $12m. Country B is the lowest with sales worth $5m.

But how does this information help CC decide where to open more outlets?

- Option 1: CC should open more shops in country C, where sales are the highest at $18m. Customers like their products so this could mean increased revenue.

- Option 2: CC might not have enough shops in countries B, D and A, and this might be why the value of sales is only $5m, $6m and $8m. If CC opened more shops in these countries, more customers could access their products.

(NOTE: based on the data, each option is feasible.)

How else could the same information be presented? Charts are used to present a group of related facts graphically. Examples include bar charts, pie charts and line graphs.

Bar charts

These show data in bars or columns. The higher the column height, the greater the value.

Bar charts are a useful method when there is a single variable, for example, revenue each month. Bar charts:

- ✓ are easy to construct
- ✗ only show a small number of simple figures.

Pie charts

These show proportions – how much one part is of the whole.

Pie charts are useful for simple comparisons between different options for the same question. Pie charts are:

- ✓ easy for seeing results quickly
- ✗ only present percentages – no actual totals.

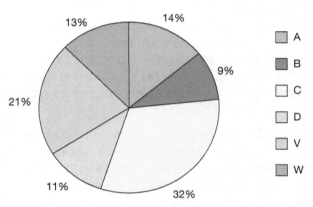

Figure 11.02 A pie chart showing Cool Clothing's sales value in each country.

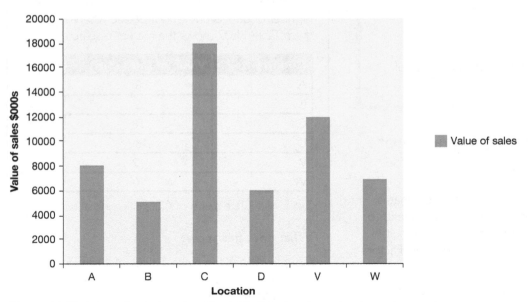

Figure 11.01 A bar chart showing Cool Clothing's sales value in each country.

Line graphs

These show the relationship between two sets of numbers.

Line graphs are useful for showing trends over time, for example, between value of sales or between country. Line graphs:

✓ make it easy to spot trends quickly

✗ only give a limited amount of information.

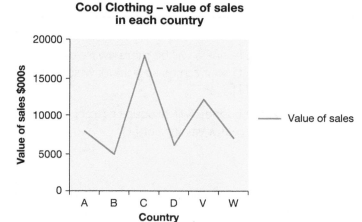

Figure 11.03 A line graph showing Cool Clothing's sales value in each country.

Other methods include **pictograms**. Data is represented by symbols of the item being displayed. Pictograms are:

✓ good for visual impact

✗ difficult to represent exact numbers.

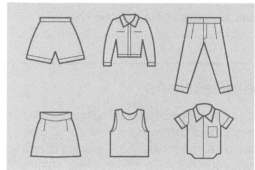

Figure 11.04 A pictogram showing Cool Clothing's products.

TIP Say what you can see. Use numbers to support what you are saying. This shows that you are applying your knowledge.

Sample question

Vikram is a farmer. He grows and sells fresh fruit and vegetables to local markets. Vikram cannot decide whether to focus on fruit or vegetables.

Identify **two** changes shown in Figure 11.05. Explain how Vikram can use this information to help him make his decision. **[6]**

Sample answer:

Change 1: Sales of vegetables have increased from $30 000 to $45 000 in three years. Selling more vegetables could widen his customer base, leading to more sales. **[3]**

Change 2: Sales of fruit have fallen by about $8000 over the same time. Fewer people want Vikram's fruit, compared to vegetables. **[3]**

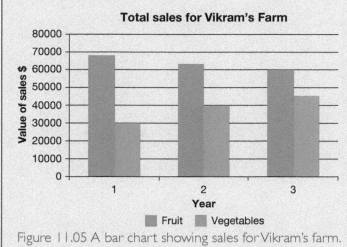

Figure 11.05 A bar chart showing sales for Vikram's farm.

Progress check

1 Define 'focus group'.

2 How can bias be a problem?

3 Why is sampling used?

4 State **one** advantage of using a pie chart.

Summary

There are many methods of market research that a business can use. Each method has its advantages and limitations. The results of market research can be presented in many different ways.

Sample questions

SRT makes a wide range of paints. These are sold to other businesses and customers in many countries. Market research is important. The Managing Director said, 'Different countries have different legal standards for paint. Customers want different colours and size of tins.' SRT uses the services of many businesses from the tertiary sector (see 2.01).

Example 1:
Define 'market research'. [2]

Sample answer:
This is the process of collecting and analysing information [1] about customers or a market [1].

Example 2:
Outline **two** advantages to SRT of using market research. [4]

Sample answer:
Advantage 1: the business will be more aware of customer needs [1] so it can make colours which the customers want [1].

Advantage 2: the business will produce correct amounts [1], so avoid wasting paint [1].

Example 3:
Explain **two** possible methods of market research that SRT could use. Which method do you think SRT should choose? Justify your answer. [6]

Sample answer:
Information from trade organisation [1] data is relevant to the paint industry [1]. A focus group allows in-depth views to be collected [1] so the business is able to know what its customers in different countries want [1]. Both give relevant information, but trade organisation data can be out of date so using a focus group might be better [1]. It might cost more but will be more detailed and relevant to SRT's needs [1].

Examination-style questions

JUG makes a range of soft drinks. It wants to create a new range of healthy drinks for older people. JUG's marketing department has carried out a questionnaire. This is shown in Table 11.03. It also plans to use some secondary market research to reduce the cost.

	Men's preference	Women's preference
Water	100	270
Fruit drinks	230	400
Milk	260	150
Fizzy drinks	230	60
Other	180	120

Table 11.03 Extract of results from questionnaire (sample of 2000 people).

a   Identify **two** reasons why market research might not be useful.
Reason 1:
Reason 2:   [2]

b   Using the information, draw a graph or chart to show the results of this question for fruit drinks and fizzy drinks.   [4]

> **TIP**
>
> If you have to draw a chart or table, remember to label the lines and give the chart a title.

c   Explain **two** ways that JUG could use the market research information to help make marketing decisions.
Way 1:
Way 2:   [8]

d   Consider the advantages and disadvantages of the following **three** methods of secondary market research JUG could use. Which method do you think it should use? Justify your answer.
Government sources:
Internet research:
Commercial market research reports:
Recommendation: [12]

Marketing mix: product and price

The marketing mix is the combination of product, price, place and promotion used to sell its products. Another name for it is the **Four Ps.**

12.01 Product

Getting the product right is important. People must have something to buy. Without a product, there is no need for the other elements of the marketing mix.

> **TIP**
> The word 'product' can refer either to goods (physical items) or services (for example, transport).

12.02 The costs and benefits of developing new products

A business cannot always offer the same product. At some point it must innovate to keep up with or stay ahead of the competition.

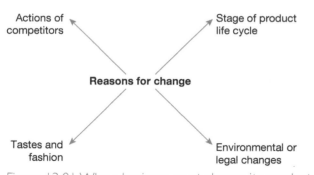

Figure 12.01 Why a business must change its products.

Benefits of new product development	Costs of new product development
• Maintain customer loyalty	• Cost of market research
• Target new markets or segments – increase sales	• Development costs – new equipment and training
• Competitive advantage if first – can use price skimming	• Marketing costs to launch product
• Diversification so spread risk	• Risk to image if product 'fails'

Table 12.01 Benefits and costs of new product development.

12.03 Brand image

It is not just buying a product that matters, but what customers think it represents.

A brand name helps to distinguish a product from other similar products. A business wants the name to stick in the customer's mind so that they continue to buy their product – the business needs to develop **brand loyalty**. If customers trust the brand, they are more likely to try new products the business provides. Prices can be set higher than less well-known brands without damaging sales.

> **TIP**
> A brand name can be a product (for example, iPod) or business name (for example, Nike).

Brand image: how a product is perceived by customers.

Brand name: special or unique name by which the product or company is known.

12.04 The role of packaging

Packaging is more than just a container for a product. It has the following features and purposes:

- **Protect** – to keep the product in perfect condition.
- **Provide information** – so that customers know how to use the product.
- **Legal requirement** – it will include safety details to protect users.
- **Attract customers** – the colour and shape can help a product stand out against the competition.
- **Boost brand image** – luxury products are expected to have expensive packaging.
- **Extend product life** – new packaging can remind/ attract customers.

12.05 The product life cycle

A product will pass through many stages, from when it first appears in a market to when the business decides to stop selling it.

→ All products go through the same stages. How long each stage lasts is different. Some products might be unsuccessful so go straight from introduction to decline.

→ A business with many products has many different product life cycles to manage.

TERM

Product life cycle: the stages a product will pass through, from its introduction to growth to the end of the product's time in the market.

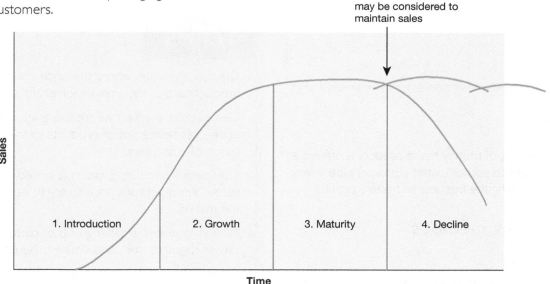

Extension strategies may be considered to maintain sales

1. Introduction **2. Growth** **3. Maturity** **4. Decline**

Sales (y-axis) **Time** (x-axis)

1. Product not well known. Lots of advertising, and prices may be low to attract attention.

2. Sales rise quickly. Prices may rise in line with any competitors. Promotion used to encourage repeat purchase and attract new customers.

3. Product widely available. Prices similar to competitors. Should have brand loyalty. Promotion tries to remind customers.

4. Sales fall. Prices may be lowered. Limited, if any, promotion done. Need to decide whether to keep/ stop product.

Figure 12.02 The product life cycle.

How stages of product life cycle can influence marketing decisions

Decisions will change at each stage for different products. Actions will be influenced by factors such as marketing objectives, customer behaviour and competitor reactions.

Extension strategies

As a product approaches the decline stage, a business might try to boost its sales and slow its rate of decline.

Strategies include the following:

- Sell the product to a new market.
- Target a different market segment.
- Add new features to 'improve' the product.
- Change the packaging to change its image.
- Encourage customers to use the product more often.

TIP

Do not confuse these strategies with general promotion techniques such as lower prices or more advertising.

12.06 Price

Price is the amount of money that a product is offered at. This should take into account what customers are willing to pay while allowing the business to make a profit.

12.07 Pricing methods

Cost plus pricing

Some businesses want to make sure the price covers its costs and makes a profit. Cost plus pricing:

- ✓ is quick and simple to calculate
- ✓ covers costs
- ✓ ensures a profit on each unit
- ✗ might not be competitive if the price is too high – sales could drop.

Worked example

BYC makes specialist bicycles. Each one costs $500 to build and BYC adds 50% to the total cost to calculate the selling price. What is the selling price?

1   Cost + 50%

2   $500 + (500 \times 0.5) = $750

Competitive pricing

The price set is based on what the competition is charging. With competitive pricing:

- ✓ the price is similar to rivals so possible to maintain sales
- ✓ customers have a lot of choice, which is useful in a competitive market
- ✗ competitor actions have a major impact on the business's marketing strategy
- ✗ there is limited control over price
- ✗ there is no guarantee of profit
- ✗ the business needs another way to attract customers.

TERMS

Cost plus pricing: where the price covers cost of production plus set amount for profit.

Competitive market: where there are many businesses selling similar products to the same group of customers.

Competitive pricing: product is priced at or just below a competitor's price to try to gain more of the market.

Market segment: smaller group of customers with similar characteristics and similar product needs.

Penetration pricing: setting a very low price to enter a new market.

Price skimming: setting a high price for a new product.

Promotional pricing: when prices are reduced for a limited period of time to boost sales.

Penetration pricing

This is a good way to enter a new (or competitive) market. Once the product is established, prices are often increased. With penetration pricing:

✓ low prices can attract customers

✓ market share can be increased quickly

✗ there is a possible loss of revenue as prices are set lower

✗ the price might not cover costs, so this is not a long-term option

✗ it might take a long time to recover development costs

✗ customers might buy from rivals if the business tries to increase the price.

Price skimming

Some customers will pay more to have the latest product. Prices can be lowered later to widen the market and maintain the level of sales. With this method:

✓ the business recovers development costs quicker due to high price

✓ the quality image for the product is reinforced

✗ not everyone can afford the high price, so the business could lose sales

✗ when rivals enter the market, they could undercut the business and sales could fall.

Promotional pricing

Changing the price for a limited period of time can encourage customers to switch from a competitor. This method:

✓ attracts customers who might continue to buy products later

✓ boosts sales as part of growth strategy

✓ helps to sell unwanted/old inventory

✗ could reduce revenue as the business receives less money per item.

12.08 Price elasticity of demand

An important factor affecting demand is the price of the product. Price elasticity focuses on the extent to which demand is affected by a change in price.

TERMS

Price elastic: a change in price leading to a larger change in demand.

Price elasticity of demand: the responsiveness of demand for a product as a result of a change in the price.

Price inelastic: a change in price leading to a smaller change in demand.

Price elastic	Price inelastic
Demand is more responsive to change in price.	Demand is less responsive to change in price.
If prices rise:	If prices rise:
• demand will fall by more than percentage change in price	• demand will fall by less than percentage change in price
• revenue is likely to fall.	• revenue is likely to rise.
If prices fall:	If prices fall:
• demand will rise by more than percentage change in price	• demand will rise by less than percentage change in price
• revenue is likely to rise.	• revenue is likely to fall.
Example: product with many alternatives.	Examples: where there are few substitutes, for example, luxury or branded items.

Table 12.02 The features of price elasticity and price inelasticity.

TIP

You do not have to do any elasticity calculation. Think about how elasticity affects the demand for different products.

Sample question

Rosa makes handmade luxury shoes. As it is a niche market, Rosa believes that demand is price inelastic. Material costs have increased. Rosa plans to increase prices to maintain profits.

Outline the effect on Rosa's business if she increases prices. [4]

Sample answer:
As demand is inelastic, sales of shoes should fall by less than the percentage change in price. Rosa should be able to recover the extra money spent due to the increase in cost of materials. **[4]**

Progress check

1 State **two** brand names that you really like. What attracts you to these products?

2 Name the main stages of the product life cycle.

3 State **one** situation when cost plus pricing is useful.

4 If price were lowered for a price inelastic product, would sales rise or fall?

Summary

Brand image and packaging are important. The different stages of the product life cycle have implications in terms of costs, sales and profit. A business has a choice of pricing methods. Each one has advantages and disadvantages, so the context will help determine the method. Price elasticity of demand will have an impact on sales and profit.

Sample questions

GPS produces a wide range of sports-based computer games. It is a competitive market. The Marketing Director has been looking at information for two products.

Game C: is in maturity stage of product life cycle. It is sold in most retailer shops. Demand is believed to be price elastic.

Game D: is about to be released. It has been expensive to make as it includes the latest graphics. Demand is expected to be very high. GPS cannot decide whether to use price skimming or not.

Example 1:
Do you think price skimming is the best method of pricing for GPS to use for Game D? Justify your answer. **[6]**

Sample answer:
High cost can deter some customers **[1]** so the business risks making less revenue **[1]** but will be able to cover development costs quicker. This is important as technology changes quickly **[1]**, otherwise the costs will not be recovered **[1]**. Customers will pay for the latest graphics so it may be sensible to make money while the business can **[1]**, before competitors produce alternative goods **[1]**.

Example 2:
Explain **two** ways in which the stage of the product life cycle might influence the decisions GPS makes about product C. **[8]**

Sample answer:
Way 1: Promotion **[1]**: as the product is in maturity stage, sales are likely to drop. GPS might want to remind customers that it is still available in most shops **[1]**. Using advertisements in computer magazines **[1]** to highlight key features of the product could encourage people to keep buying it **[1]**.

Way 2: Price **[1]**: this is likely to be similar to other sports games in the market **[1]**. As demand is price elastic **[1]**, GPS could offer discounts, especially as any reduction should lead to a greater increase in sales **[1]**.

Examination-style questions

MHC makes a wide range of electrical products including cameras and phones. It is a competitive market. All of its products are sold in its distinctive red packaging. The Operations Director knows brand image is important. He thinks product X, its best-selling phone, is in the decline stage of the product life cycle. He cannot decide whether to develop a new product or use extension strategies. One option is to start selling its products in new foreign markets.

a   Define 'product life cycle'.   [2]

b   Outline **two** reasons why packaging might be important for MHC.
Reason 1:
Reason 2:   [4]

c   Explain **one** advantage and **one** disadvantage to MHC of developing new products.
Advantage:
Disadvantage: [6]

d   Explain **two** benefits to MHC of product X having a positive brand image.
Benefit 1:
Benefit 2:   [8]

e   Explain how the following **three** extension strategies might help MHC increase sales. Which strategy do you think MHC should use? Justify your answer.
Target different market segment:
Add new features:
Change packaging:
Recommendation: [12]

Marketing mix: place and promotion

13.01 Place – channels of distribution

Decisions have to be made about where and how the product will be sold.

There are four main ways in which goods reach consumers.

In Figure 13.01, channels 2 to 4 are indirect as intermediaries (or 'middlemen') are used to get the products to the consumer.

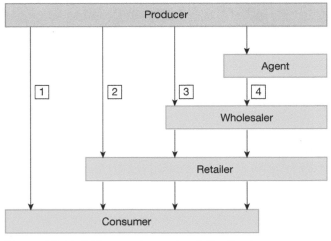

Figure 13.01 Different channels of distribution.

Channel 1: Producer → consumer

This is the only direct channel. The producer sells its products direct to the customer. This is often used when one business sells to another business. Other examples include factory shops and e-commerce.

Advantages	Disadvantages
• It is the quickest channel. • The producer receives direct feedback from consumers. • The producer makes all profit on sales.	• Access is difficult for consumers if they are not near the producer. • There is a smaller potential market as fewer people are aware of products. • There are additional time and costs of distribution such as transport, orders for producer.

Table 13.01 Advantages and disadvantages of Channel 1.

Channel 2: Producer → retailer → consumer

Larger retailers can act as their own wholesalers. A business buys products directly from the producer and sells them to consumers.

Advantages	Disadvantages
• The retailer can benefit from discounts for bulk buying. • The retailer does the advertising. • The producer receives feedback direct from retailer.	• Retailers need space to store large quantities of goods. • Retailers have to pay transport costs. • The retailer might want additional influence over what products are produced.

Table 13.02 Advantages and disadvantages of Channel 2.

Channel 3: Producer ➔ wholesaler ➔ retailer ➔ consumer

This is the traditional method used by many small and medium-sized businesses.

Advantages	Disadvantages
• The producer does not have to deal with lots of retailers – this means less paperwork.	• The producer has no direct contact with customers, so relies on feedback from others.
• Less storage space is required.	• The producer makes less profit as there are many links in the distribution channel.
• The wholesaler carries the risk of unsold inventory, not the producer.	
• The wholesaler provides choice to the retailers.	• The producer has limited influence over marketing decisions.
• Retailers can buy the amount needed.	• Higher price for consumers as both retailer and wholesalers need to make a profit.
• The wholesaler has contacts, increasing potential market.	• It can take a long time for goods to reach the consumer. For perishable products, poorer quality could damage the producer's reputation.
• The wholesaler can offer credit terms, helping cash flow.	

Table 13.03 Advantages and disadvantages of Channel 3.

Note: some wholesalers also allow consumers to buy directly from them.

Channel 4: Producer ➔ agent ➔ wholesaler ➔ retailer ➔ consumer

Agents are often used when a business wants to sell abroad.

Advantages	Disadvantages
Agents provide local knowledge of laws, customs and markets.	There is increased cost as another intermediary is used.
	There is limited influence over the marketing mix.

Table 13.04 Advantages and disadvantages of Channel 4.

13.02 The difference between a wholesaler and agent

A wholesaler buys products in large quantities from the producer, and resells smaller quantities of the goods to retailers or consumers. This is called **breaking bulk**. Wholesalers receive a discount from producers for bulk buying.

An agent does not buy the goods, but will usually receive a commission for every sale arranged.

TERMS

Place: where the product is sold and the methods used to get the product there.

Channel of distribution: how goods and services get from the producer to the consumer.

Wholesaler: a business person (intermediary) who buys goods from a producer to sell to the retailer or customer.

13.03 Factors to consider when choosing a channel of distribution

- **Cost** – of storage, administration, transport and advertising.

- **Nature of the product** – perishable and fragile goods must be moved quickly and carefully. Technical or specialist products may need to offer personal service.

- **Brand image** – method must match perceived image, for example, luxury.

- **The market** – is it a mass or niche market? Is it sold locally, nationally or in other countries?

- **Size of the business** – does the business have the structure, expertise and finance to avoid need for intermediaries? Does the business want control over how or where the product is distributed?

13.04 Promotion

Aims of promotion

Promotion is all about increasing sales. This can be done by:

- **informing** customers about products
- **raising awareness** of new products or features
- **persuading** customers to buy or switch from rival products
- **reminding** customers about existing products
- **improving** brand image.

Methods of promotion

> **TIP**
> Promotion means more than just advertising.

A business will use a range of promotion methods to ensure (current and potential) customers know about their products.

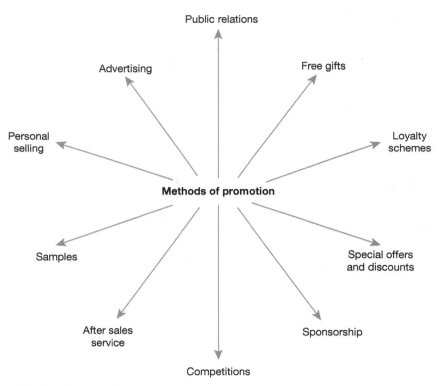

Figure 13.02 Different methods of promotion.

Method	How it influences sales
Point of sale displays	These are designed to highlight the product so it stands out from rivals. Can encourage impulse purchases.
Competitions	Customers can be tempted to buy the product so that they have a chance to win something.
Free gifts	Items given away with product. Collections encourage people to continue buying the product to complete a set.
After sales service	Guarantees, repair service or helpline provided to reassure customers.
Loyalty schemes	Consumers collect points or rewards for each purchase. This encourages repeat purchases.

Table 13.05 How different sales promotion methods influence sales.

13.07 Other methods of promotion

Method	How it influences sales
Public relations	Effectively free publicity. The business tries to build an image by getting positive stories published or known to customers.
Sponsorship	The business gives money or support to an event, project or people. Business/product name will be linked to sponsorship to increase attention. This can be used to target market segments or promote certain image.
Celebrity endorsement	Associating the name of a product or business with a well-known person. Interest in the well-known person can boost product image and sales.
Personal selling	A salesperson or agent talks directly to customers to get them to buy. This helps to build customer relationships.

Table 13.06 How other methods of promotion influence sales.

TERMS

Promotion: all activities that are designed to make customers aware of their products so that they are encouraged to buy them.

Informative advertising: any advertising which gives people information about a product.

Persuasive advertising: any advertising which tries to convince people that they need or want the product.

13.05 Advertising

Advertising (also known as 'above the line promotion') can be either informative or persuasive.

Informative advertising
This allows customers to base decisions on facts provided. Websites, newspapers, magazines, posters and leaflets are useful for reference.

Persuasive advertising
Most advertisements are persuasive. Visual methods such as television have more impact. This attracts attention. There are other traditional ways to advertise such as newspaper, radio, billboards and leaflets. Increasingly, social media and websites are being used.

13.06 Sales promotion

Sales promotions (also known as 'below the line promotions') try to persuade customers to buy products now rather than later. Unlike advertising, sales promotions are aimed specifically at the target market.

Method	How it influences sales
Discounts and special offers, for example, discount coupons Buy One Get One Free (BOGOF)	Short-term influence as this is only available for limited period. Customers are attracted as they think the product represents better value for money.
Free samples	Smaller versions of product are given to tempt people to try product first and encourage them to buy.

73

13.08 Factors to consider when choosing a method of promotion

- **Marketing budget** – what can the business afford to spend? Money spent on promotion cannnot then be used for other purposes.

- **Marketing strategy** – what objectives have the business set?

- **Type of product** – customers might need information for technical or specialised products before they feel confident to buy it.

- **Stage in product life cycle** – introducing a new product will need a lot of promotion.

- **Target market** – mass market or niche markets need different approaches. Is it to be sold worldwide, nationally or locally?

- **What are competitors doing?**

Sample question

Any Baked (AB) makes a range of products from cakes to breads. The products are sold in a variety of shops and supermarkets in country J. The Marketing Director wants to increase sales. She cannot decide on the best method of promotion to use.

Explain how each of the following **three** methods of promotion could help AB increase its sales:

- free samples
- display in shops
- discounts

Which method do you think AB should use? Justify your answer. [12]

Sample answer:
Free samples: They could let people try the bread, and if they liked it then sales might increase. Without knowing what it tastes like, it is difficult to persuade people to buy it, as flavour and taste are important. If less popular breads are given as samples as well, this is a good way to increase interest in them.

Display in shops: As customers walk past, it reminds them about AB's products. If they cannot see what they want, they are not likely to buy it. But there might not be room for a display in all

the shops: not everyone would be made aware, so sales might not increase everywhere.

Discounts: Customers can be attracted by cheaper prices and buy the business's cakes rather than other brands. Customers might then still buy them after the price has gone back to its usual level. Shops would be happy as lower prices might bring in more customers, who then buy other things as well. However, a lower price might suggest lower quality and damage AB's reputation.

Conclusion: I would recommend free samples as people like to try things before they buy them. Discounts would lower revenue so AB would have to sell even more to cover the cost. Displays can attract attention but because the product is food, people are more likely to buy it if they already know that they like it.

> **TIP**
>
> Unless the question is specifically about advertising, try to cover two different forms of promotion.

13.09 The importance of a marketing budget

A marketing budget includes the costs of advertising, free gifts and website development, as well as the cost of marketing employees and office space.

All marketing costs time and money, so it is important to make the best use of resources. It needs to be cost-effective. To know this, a business should:

- set a marketing objective, for example, increase sales by $5000

- check how much time and money has been spent, for example, $3000 on advertising

- measure results.

> **TERM**
>
> Marketing budget: the money set aside by a business to promote its products and services for a given period of time.

13.10 Technology and the marketing mix

Technology has had an impact on marketing. New products are always being developed. Pricing strategies can be constantly updated based on spending patterns, as more data is available. Customers no longer have to visit shops or even be in the same country to purchase products. Promotion can be targeted more easily to specific customer groups.

E-commerce

More goods and services are being bought and sold online. Businesses have to think about how best to attract customers' attention to their website, and how to get products safely and securely to customers anywhere in the world.

> **TERM**
>
> E-commerce: the process of buying and selling over the internet.

Opportunities of e-commerce	Threats of e-commerce
For businesses: • lower fixed costs • better information • increased target market.	**For businesses:** • increased global competition • cost of maintaining website • not everyone has internet access • higher distribution costs.
For consumers: • can place orders when they want • more choice • lower prices • more information.	**For consumers:** • cannot see before buying • lack of personal service • fear of hacking • returning unwanted/ damaged goods can be difficult.

Table 13.07 Opportunities and threats of e-commerce to businesses and consumers.

Use of the internet and social media networks for promotion

The rise of social media networks such as Facebook and Twitter have altered how products are advertised, and how customer opinions can be gained. Businesses can gain instant feedback from potential customers, wherever they live.

Social media networks can help generate immediate interest. Websites, sponsored links and pop-up adverts allow businesses to better target customers.

Progress check

1 Which is the most direct channel of distribution?

2 When is an agent likely to be used?

3 Outline **two** factors to consider when deciding on a method of promotion.

4 Outline **two** ways in which technology has changed marketing.

Summary

There are four main channels of distribution, each with its own advantages and disadvantages. There are important differences between the various types of promotion. For every situation, a choice of distribution channels and promotional strategies is possible.

Sample questions

Otto owns a small shop in a town centre. He sells a range of luxury products including handmade bags and gloves. He buys all his inventory from a wholesaler. Otto wants to increase sales, but he does not have a marketing strategy. He wants to promote his goods, and has a marketing budget of $200.

Example 1:
Define 'promotion'. **[2]**

Sample answer:
Promotion refers to all activities that are designed to make customers aware of their products **[1]** so that they are encouraged to buy **[1]**.

Example 2:
Outline **two** advantages to Otto of using a wholesaler. **[4]**

Sample answer:
Advantage 1: no need to store a lot of inventory **[1]** as he only has a small shop **[1]**.

Advantage 2: more choice **[1]** so Otto can select different makes of bags **[1]**.

Examination-style questions

KLH owns a chain of 40 hotels in different countries. 70% of its guests are business people. KLH has a good reputation and offers competitive prices. The Marketing Director is looking at ways to increase the level of sales. She has a marketing budget of $3m. She said, 'Technology has changed our business. Having a website is very helpful – and not just for advertising and promotion.' KLH has plans to open ten more hotels in the next two years. KLH's Directors know that finding the right locations will be important.

a   Define 'marketing budget'. [2]

b   Outline **two** ways in which technology might influence the marketing mix for KLH.
Way 1:
Way 2: [4]

c   Explain **two** methods of advertising (other than using a website) KLH might use.
Method 1:
Method 2: [8]

d   KLH is planning to use the website for all its promotion. Do you think this is a good idea? Justify your answer. [6]

Marketing strategy

Learning summary

By the end of this unit you should understand:

- [ ] marketing strategies
- [ ] nature and impact of legal controls relating to marketing
- [ ] opportunities and problems of entering new foreign markets.

14.01 Choosing a marketing strategy

A business must choose the right combination of all four parts of the marketing mix (4 Ps) to market and sell its products.

The mix will change over time, and vary for every business as marketing objectives are based on business objectives. See Table 14.01 for examples.

Business objective	Marketing objective
Grow sales by 15%	Develop new products
	Target new markets
Increase profits	Increase prices
	Reduce marketing budget, for example, less promotion

Table 14.01 Examples of business and marketing objectives.

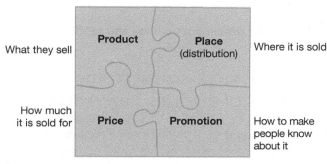

Figure 14.01 Combining the four parts of the marketing mix to create a strategy.

TIP Objectives can be used to measure success, to judge whether the marketing has been cost-effective.

TERM

Marketing strategy: a plan of actions a business will take to achieve its marketing objectives.

Figure 14.02 How business objectives can influence marketing strategy.

14.02 Impact of legal controls on marketing strategy

A business has to be careful about what they claim a product can do and what they offer. Legal controls exist to protect consumers against misleading promotion, and faulty and dangerous goods.

For a business, this can increase its costs. Products must be safe and fit for purpose. Breaking the law can lead to fines and the need to replace products. It can also damage their brand image.

Sample question

Dwayne is a qualified teacher. He wants to set up a home tutoring business. He has carried out some market research. His target market is 14–16-year-old IGCSE students. Dwayne knows he will have to build customer relationships if he is to be successful. He is not sure how legal controls will affect any marketing decisions.

Outline how legal controls might affect the marketing decisions of Dwayne's business. [4]

Sample answer:
Legal controls will influence how Dwayne does his advertising, as he must avoid misleading people about what the students can achieve from his tutoring service. He cannot claim to have guaranteed A* grades for all his customers, as he has not started his business yet.

14.03 Opportunities and problems of entering new foreign markets

Many businesses no longer want to sell their products only in their own (home) country.

Opportunities

- **Increased target market** – potentially higher sales and revenue.

- **Spread risk** – the business will be less reliant on the home market for all its sales. The home market might have no more scope for growth.

- **Fewer trade restrictions** – it is now possible to trade in more countries.

- **Greater recognition** – this can improve brand image.

Problems of entering foreign markets

Buying and selling overseas is not the same as trading in home markets. This is a list of potential problems:

- **Lack of knowledge of local markets** – customs, traditions, laws and trading practices can be different.

- **Lack of contacts** – the business will need to know where the best locations are, which products to sell and how to market the products.

- **National cultures and tastes differ** – other countries may not like the business's products.

- **Additional costs** – transport, labelling and promotional costs need to be paid.

- **Language problems** – is there a common language, or does the business have people who can translate for them?

- **Government rules and regulations.**

- **Reaction of competitors in overseas markets** – other businesses are likely to react to the threat of competition to try to protect their sales.

- **Exchange rates, import quotas and tariffs.**

14.04 Methods to overcome problems of entering new markets

Rather than use e-commerce or sell directly to another country, many businesses involve other people or businesses to help sell their products. These people can offer the local knowledge needed. The choice of method can depend on factors such as the market, what the product is, cost and control.

Options include:

1. **Joint venture** – two businesses pooling their resources together on a specific project (see 4.07).

Advantages	Disadvantages
• Access to other markets and distribution channels.	• Objectives might not be clearly set out and communicated to everyone.
• Less risk as the business shares costs with other business.	• The business will have to share profits.
• Access to new technology, expertise and knowledge.	• Different objectives, cultures and management styles can affect level of cooperation.
• Some countries only allow foreign businesses access if they work with local business.	• There can be disagreements if one party provides more expertise, finance than the other.

Table 14.02 Advantages and disadvantages of joint ventures.

2 **International franchising** – this allows a business to trade under the name of another business to sell its products (see 4.07).

3 **Licensing** –a business allows its products to be made by another business in another country. This can saves transport costs, but it can be difficult to control quality.

4 **Use an agent** –agents use their contacts and knowledge to find customers, but will expect a commission from all sales. Changes in exchange rates or import controls can also be a problem.

Progress check

1 What are the four elements of the marketing mix?

2 Identify **two** marketing objectives that a business might have.

3 Which is the most important element of the marketing mix? Explain.

4 Name **two** opportunities of international trade.

Sample question

JGR makes a range of food products for babies. It wants to start selling its products in country K, which has a growing population. The Marketing Director is worried as there are many problems to overcome. She said, 'We need to find out which product they like. Legal issues mean we cannot open our own factory there.'

Explain **two** possible methods JGR could use to overcome the problems of entering country K. **[6]**

Sample answer:

Method 1: Produce goods under licence – a local manufacturer could then make the food for them so JGR does not have to worry about having its own factory. **[3]**

Method 2: Form a joint venture with a local business. They are likely to have knowledge of the local tastes, which would save JGR from having to carry out market research. **[3]**

Summary

A marketing strategy tries to help a business achieve its marketing objectives. Selecting the right combination of price, product, promotion and place will depend on what the objective is in a given situation. Like most business activities, legal controls will influence marketing decisions and actions. Entering new foreign markets offers many opportunities for businesses, but there are also problems which have to be overcome as well.

Sample questions

Otto owns a small shop in a town centre. He sells a range of luxury products including handmade bags and gloves. He buys all his inventory from a wholesaler. Otto wants to increase sales, but he does not have a marketing strategy. He wants to do some promotion and has a marketing budget of $200.

Example 1
Identify **two** possible marketing objectives that a business might have. **[2]**

Sample answer:
Objective 1: Increase market share to 3%.

Objective 2: Increase profit by 10%.

> **TIP**
> General answers are acceptable if the type of business is not named in the question.

Example 2:
Outline **two** possible advantages to Otto of having a marketing strategy. **[4]**

Sample answer:
Advantage 1: it provides a sense of direction **[1]** so he will know whether or not he increased sales **[1]**.

Advantage 2: it helps with making marketing decisions **[1]**, so Otto can choose which method of promotion is more appropriate **[1]**.

Example 3:
Explain **two** possible elements of Otto's marketing strategy. **[6]**

Sample answer:
Element 1: Cost plus pricing – as he is selling luxury goods, customers might be willing to pay more, so he can guarantee himself some profit on all items sold. **[3]**

Element 2: His business could provide sponsorship of a fashion event. His name could be linked to the event, increasing attention. **[3]**

Examination-style questions

Kallis Engineering [KE] is a private limited company. It is a small engineering business based in South Africa. It makes farm equipment including tractors and trailers. The Finance Director wants to raise an additional $20m in finance as KE plans to expand by selling its equipment in Asia. She said, 'This is a very competitive market, but with the right marketing strategy I think this can work.' She also knows that there are benefits to trading overseas.

a   Define 'marketing strategy'. [2]

b   Outline **two** reasons why KE might want to sell products in new foreign markets.

Reason 1:
Reason 2:   [4]

c   Explain **two** possible elements of KE's marketing strategy.
Element 1:
Element 2:   [8]

d   State the advantages and disadvantages of the following **three** methods KE could use to enter a new foreign market. Which method do you think KE should use? Justify your answer.
Agent:
Joint venture:
Licensing:
Recommendation: [12]

Section 4:
OPERATIONS MANAGEMENT

Production of goods and services

15.01 The meaning of production

Production is an important way for businesses to add value (see 1.05).

Managing resources effectively means:

- ensuring that enough products are available when required to meet customer needs

- finding the right combination of resources and method of production to be cost-effective.

How production is carried out depends on what product is produced, the amount needed, the factors of production available and the method of production chosen.

Production can be either:

- **capital-intensive** – using a high proportion of machinery to produce goods

- **labour-intensive** – using a high proportion of labour to produce goods.

TERM

Production: the process of converting raw materials or components into finished goods.

15.02 Difference between production and productivity

The level of production refers to the amount of output. Productivity is the rate at which goods are produced in a given period of time.

Productivity can be calculated in a number of ways:

TIP

Include the relevant formula as part of your answer in any calculation questions.

Worked example

A factory employs 50 workers. Annual output is 8250 units in 2016. What is the productivity per employee?

Formula $\dfrac{8250}{50}$ Answer = 165 (units per employee)

- This information can be used to compare performance over time or against similar businesses. The higher the figure, the higher the level of productivity.

- A business will aim for **lower average costs** and **higher productivity**.

By labour	By machine	By hours
$\dfrac{\text{Total output}}{\text{Number of employees}}$	$\dfrac{\text{Total output}}{\text{Number of machines}}$	$\dfrac{\text{Total output}}{\text{Number of hours}}$

Table 15.01 Different ways of calculating productivity.

15.03 Benefits of increasing efficiency and how to achieve it

Making better use of resources should help lower the average cost.

How to increase efficiency

- **Redesign factory layout or tasks** to remove unnecessary movement or stages.

- **Improving labour skills** could mean fewer mistakes. The cost of training should be covered by increased output, less wastage or better reputation.

- **Update old technology or automate** – new machines are less likely to break down. Replacing employees with machines could allow continuous production.

- **Improve motivation** so that employees are more productive.

- **Introduce lean production methods** so that the business uses as few resources as necessary.

Sample question

TXW makes car parts which are sold to other businesses. The Production manager has been looking at productivity data. This is shown in Table 15.02. All employees work a 40-hour week.

Year	Number of employees	Output per week (units)	Output per employee per week (units)
2016	200	23 000	115
2015	250	27 000	108

Table 15.02 Productivity data for TXW.

Explain **two** possible reasons why productivity changed in 2016. **[6]**

Sample answer:
Reason 1: new machines which don't break down as often so productivity increased by 7 cars per employee. **[3]**

Reason 2: Training so employees are able to produce more parts in the same period of time. **[3]**

15.04 Why businesses hold inventories

Inventory can be raw materials, part-made goods or finished products ready to be sold. A business tries to minimise costs but still have enough inventory to maintain production and be able to meet customer demands.

Advantages	Disadvantages
• Can always meet orders	• Higher costs of storage and insurance
• Avoid supply issues	• Risk of obsolescence (no longer wanted) and damage
• No production delays	• Opportunity cost (see 1.02) – as working capital tied up
• Economies of scale if buy in bulk	

Table 15.03 Advantages and disadvantages of holding inventory.

15.05 Concept of lean production

Using fewer resources and eliminating waste should help a business to reduce costs. There are different methods of production to achieve this.

Just in time

Production is carefully planned, so that materials arrive only as and when they are needed. This helps reduce inventory costs. The system needs suppliers who can provide inventory as and when required. If this does not happen, production stops and orders might not be met.

✓ Less space is needed for inventory so there are lower storage costs. This can help improve cash flow.

Kaizen (continuous improvement)

The basic principle here is that 'many small changes' can have a big impact on efficiency. Everyone is encouraged always to think of ways to improve how they work.

✓ This can help increase motivation as employees are involved in the process.

Team working (cell production)

Groups of employees are given responsibility for making either parts of the product, or the whole product.

✓ This can lead to increased motivation as employees arrange how their work is organised.

TERMS

Just in time: a system where materials arrive at the right time in the production process, so inventory costs are kept to a minimum.

Kaizen: an approach where small changes are continuously being made to how work is done, in order to improve quality and efficiency.

Lean production: methods designed to eliminate waste throughout the production process.

15.06 Benefits of lean production

• Fewer resources are needed, so the unit cost is lower.

• Less risk of obsolescence and damage.

• It reduces warehouse space as less inventory is needed.

• Less operational space is needed, so rent payment is lower.

• It can help with the motivation of employees as they are involved in the process.

• It saves time so more output is possible.

15.07 The main methods of production

There are three main ways to organise how goods are made.

Job production

One product is made at a time. This method is used for one-off items such as bridges or individually made clothing.

Batch production

Each batch goes through one stage of the production process before moving onto the next stage. This is used when producing a range of designs and colours, such as shoes.

Flow production

This is also known as mass production. Products pass straight from one stage of production to the next. It is a useful system for mass market products in constant demand, such as drinks.

TERMS

Batch production: this method produces a number of similar items in groups or sets.

Flow production: this method produces large numbers of the same product continually.

Job production: this method suits making individual products as per customer requirements.

15.08 Which method of production?

Deciding which method of production to use depends on many factors, such as:

• the amount of product required

• type of product

• cost

• size of market.

	Job	Batch	Flow
Level of output	Small quantity or single items	Limited volume	Large volume
Machinery used	Some but focus is on technical expertise of employees	More emphasis on specialist machinery than job	Capital-intensive – lot of technical equipment needed
Level of variety	Very flexible – each product is unique	Some flexibility as machines can be reset between batches	Inflexible – usually a standardised product is made
Production costs	Vary with each job. High labour costs	Lower than job production. Some economies through use of lower skilled workers	High set-up costs but lower unit costs
Rate of production	Relatively slow	Variable – depends on what is made	Fast and continuous
Economies of scale	None likely	Some if materials bought in bulk	Yes, so lower unit costs
Motivation of employees	High level of job satisfaction as there is variety in the work	Some repetition so motivation can be a problem	Low, as work is repetitive
Type of employees	Highly skilled	Some skills for set task	Mainly low or unskilled, so less training needed
Other issues	Expensive to make	Storage needed for partly finished batches	If machines break down, all production stops

Table 15.04 The different methods of production.

> **TIP**
> There is no single best method of production– it depends on each situation.

Sample question

Carlos makes luxury handmade suits. He has one skilled employee to help him keep up with demand. It takes a week to make each suit.

Explain **one** advantage and **one** disadvantage to Carlos of using job production. **[6]**

Sample answer:
Advantage: He would be able to charge higher prices for suits as people are willing to pay extra for something that is unique. **[3]**

Disadvantage: There would be higher labour costs as Carlos would need to have skilled employees to ensure that the products have a luxury finish. **[3]**

15.09 How technology has changed production methods

- **Automation and mass production techniques** – machines are generally faster, more accurate and productive than people. This can lead to higher efficiency, lower unit costs, better quality, continuous production and higher output.

- **Computer-Aided Design** – software that allows technical drawings to be created, so products can be created or redesigned in 2D or 3D.

- **Computer-Aided Manufacture** – computers control machines, reducing the need for labour.

Impact of technology	
✓ Less labour needed	✗ Need to update constantly to remain competitive
✓ Higher output	✗ Job insecurity can damage motivation
✓ Better quality/few mistakes	✗ High cost to set up and maintain
✓ Reduces unit cost and time	✗ Cost of retraining or recruiting specialists

Table 15.05 The impact of technology on production methods.

Progress check

1 What does labour-intensive mean?

2 What is the purpose of lean production?

3 Which method of production is most likely to lead to problems with motivation?

4 Identify **one** way that technology has changed production.

Summary

Production should result in goods being available. A business will want to increase efficiency as this means it is making better use of limited resources. There are many ways to do this, including using lean production techniques. There are three main methods of production, and each one has its advantages and disadvantages. Technology has changed how production is carried out.

TIP

Try to avoid repeating the words in the question as part of your answer, as this does not explain the term.

Sample questions

JCF makes a range of food including biscuits and cakes, using batch production. Quality control is important. JCF has 45 employees who are always looking for ways to improve how things are done. Machines often break down. JCF has a high level of inventory. The Operations Director cannot decide whether or not introducing new technology is the best way to increase productivity.

Example 1:
Define 'batch production'. [2]

Sample answer:
Products are made as a set of items [1] of a certain amount [1].

Example 2:
Explain **two** advantages to JCF of having a high level of inventory. [8]

Sample answer:
Advantage 1: The business gains economies of scale as it can order ingredients in large quantities and get a discount, which lowers the unit cost of each biscuit made. [4]

Advantage 2: The business can avoid supply problems. Some ingredients might be difficult to obtain, which would slow down production. This could mean that orders are not met and some of the fresh ingredients might be wasted. [4]

Examination-style questions

VAB makes lorries. Most components are bought locally, including the engine and glass. Only the tyres are imported. VAB employs 250 employees in the factory and 20 office workers. Production is capital-intensive, with each employee always doing the same job. A high number of factory workers leave each year. The Operations Director wants to improve productivity. He said, 'VAB needs to be efficient to remain competitive. Rent and storage costs are too high.' He plans to introduce lean production methods.

a   Define 'capital-intensive'. [2]

b   Explain **two** ways (other than lean production) that VAB could use to increase efficiency.

Way 1:
Way 2: [6]

c   Explain **two** benefits to VAB of using lean production.
Benefit 1:
Benefit 2: [8]

d   State the advantages and disadvantages of the following **three** methods of lean production VAB could use. Which method do you think it should use? Justify your answer.
Just in time:
Cell production:
Kaizen:
Recommendation: [12]

Costs, scale of production and break-even analysis

16.01 Classification of costs

All resources cost money, from rent and materials to printing leaflets. Businesses need to work out the amount of money needed to produce its goods.

TIP Costs are listed as cash outflows in a cash flow forecast. Costs are included in the Income Statement as cost of sales (variable) or expenses (fixed costs).

16.02 Fixed costs and variable costs

Costs are classed on the basis of how they are used in production.

- **Fixed costs** – these remain the same, whether or not a business produces anything; for example, rent, insurance.

- **Variable costs** – these change with the level of production, for example, raw materials. Higher output will increase variable costs.

- **Total cost** – this is the overall cost of making a certain number of goods.

- **Average cost** – this shows how much it costs to make one product.

TIP Do not confuse total cost and average cost. As output rises, total costs will rise. Average costs might fall as output rises, due to economies of scale.

TIP Fixed cost does not start at zero, so total cost cannot start at zero.

TOTAL COSTS (TC) = FC + VC
Total costs equals the total of fixed costs and variable costs

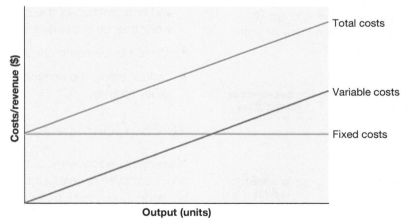

Figure 16.01 The relationship between fixed, variable and total costs.

Wages

- If employees' pay changes depending on what they do (for example, time or piece rate), their wages are variable costs.

- If employees receive a set amount every month (salary), this is seen as a fixed cost.

> ### TERMS
>
> **Average cost:** the total cost of production divided by total output.
>
> **Fixed cost:** costs that do not vary with the level of production.
>
> **Total cost:** the sum of fixed costs and variable costs added together.
>
> **Variable cost:** costs that change with the level of production.

16.03 Using cost data to make decisions

Cost information can be used to help make a number of marketing or operational decisions, such as:

- stopping or continuing production
- helping to set prices
- deciding whether or not a business should relocate
- what level of output to produce.

16.04 Economies of scale

As production increases, a business can take advantage of certain cost savings. These can lower average (or unit) costs, and are described as an economy of scale. Why does this matter? See Figure 16.02.

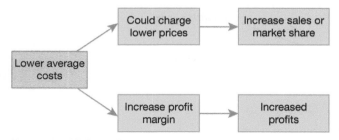

Figure 16.02 Benefits of lower average costs.

Type	How
Technical	• Can afford to buy expensive specialist equipment • Use mass production methods • Can afford to invest large sums on research and development
Financial	• Have access to more sources of finance • Larger economies of scale are seen as less risky, so lower rates of interest possible
Management	• Can afford to employ specialist managers
Marketing	• Cost of advertising is spread over more products
Purchasing	• Buy materials in bulk, accessing discounts
Risk-bearing	• Tend to operate in more than one market so the business has other markets to rely on

Table 16.01 Examples of economies of scale.

> ### TERMS
>
> **Diseconomy of scale:** factors that lead to an increase in average cost when a business grows beyond a certain size.
>
> **Economy of scale:** factors that lead to a reduction in average cost as a business increases its level of production.

16.05 Diseconomies of scale

A business can become too large to manage effectively. Unit costs can then increase, as the business experiences diseconomies of scale. For example:

- Weak coordination. As the business grows, so too will the number of departments, products, etc. The control and coordination of these can cause problems and work may be duplicated which will waste resources.

- There can be communication problems.

- Lack of employee commitment can cause motivation issues to arise.

16.06 Concept of break-even analysis

Managers need to work out how much to produce in order to cover its costs. Until this point, no profit can be made. Break-even point is the level of production where no profit or loss is made. It is reached when this formula is achieved:

$$\text{Total costs (TC)} = \text{Total revenue (TR)}$$

Break-even analysis is quick and simple to use. It helps business planning as it can:

- show the expected level of profit loss at different levels of output
- show the margin of safety (the difference between the output level and break-even output level)
- show what will happen to break-even output if costs or prices change
- support loan applications.

Worked example

GRS makes kettles. Each one sells at $25. Variable costs are $15 and fixed costs are $6000. Current output is 1000 units. The maximum factory capacity is 1200 per week.

Output	Fixed cost	Variable cost	Total cost	Total revenue	Profit
0	6000	0	6000	0	-6000
100	6000	1500	7500	2500	-5000
200	6000	3000	9000	5000	-4000
300	6000	4500	10500	7500	-3000
400	6000	6000	12000	10000	-2000
500	6000	7500	13500	12500	-1000
600	6000	9000	15000	15000	0
700	6000	10500	16500	17500	1000
800	6000	12000	18000	20000	2000
900	6000	13500	19500	22500	3000
1000	6000	15000	21000	25000	4000
1100	6000	16500	22500	27500	5000

Table 16.02 Costs data for GRS.

1 What level of output is needed for GRS to cover its costs?

Answer: Break-even output is **600** units. Selling above 600 units, GRX makes a profit. Selling below 600 units, GRS cannot cover all of its costs so a loss is made.

2 How much profit will GRS make if it produces and sells 1000 units?

Answer: $4000.

The information given in Table 16.02 can be plotted as a chart – see Figure 16.03.

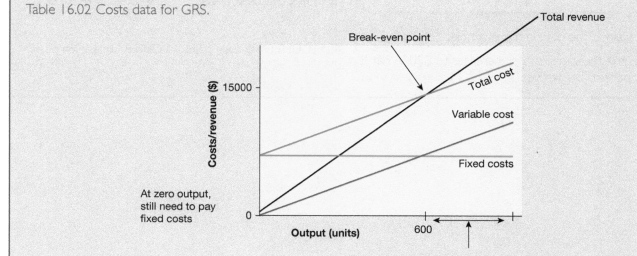

Figure 16.03 Break-even chart for GRS

TIP

If you are asked to draw a break-even chart, remember to label the lines.

Instead of using a chart, there is a formula for break-even output:

$$\frac{\text{Fixed costs}}{\text{Contribution per unit}}$$

TIP

The calculation is a quick way to check the chart.

Contribution shows the amount of revenue left from each sale that is available to go towards paying the fixed cost.

Using the worked example, the break-even output is:

$$\frac{6000}{25-15} = 600 \text{ units}$$

Any change in fixed costs, variable cost or selling price will result in a new break-even output. This will impact the level of profit (or loss).

TERM

Contribution: the selling price of the product minus the variable costs used to make it.

Look again at the data in this example.

1 Assume the variable cost increases to $20: What happens to break-even?

Contribution:

$$25 - 20 = \$5$$

Fixed costs are $6000.

Break-even point:

$$6000 / 5 = 1200 \text{ units}$$

Break-even has increased to 1200, which is the maximum number the business can make. There is no margin of safety.

2 Assume fixed costs change to $5500.

Contribution:

$$\$25 - \$15 = \$10$$

Break-even:

$$5500 / 10 = 550 \text{ units}$$

Margin of safety has increased to 450 units.

3 Price changes to $27.

Contribution:

$$\$27 - \$15 = \$12$$

Break-even:

$$6000 / 12 = 500 \text{ units}$$

Margin of safety has increased to 500 units.

Impact of price and cost changes on break-even point:

↑ Costs or ↓ prices: ↓ Costs or ↑ prices:

HIGHER break-even point   LOWER break-even point

Sample questions

Dane plans to set up a shoe repair business. His fixed costs are $120 per month and variable costs are $4. The average price of each repair is $5. Based on his market research, Dane expects to get 180 customers per month.

Example 1:
Identify **one** fixed cost and **one** variable cost that Dane might have. **[2]**

Sample answer:
Fixed cost: rent of shop.
Variable cost: glue and nails.

Example 2:
Calculate the number of shoe repairs needed each month to break even. **[2]**

Sample answer:
120 / (5-4) = 120 pairs

16.07 Limitations of break-even analysis

The calculations are based on assumptions which might not be true. Results can be misleading.

- **Not everything made is sold.** Spending patterns change or a business might hold inventory.
- **Variable costs might fall as output increases,** due to economies of scale.
- **Prices can change quickly** due to competition.
- **Fixed costs can change** as new equipment might be needed to produce more.

Summary

There are many different types of cost that a business must be aware of. Average cost is key to understanding economies and diseconomies of scale. Fixed, variable and total costs are used in break-even analysis. Break-even is a useful planning tool but it does have its limitations.

Progress check

1 What is the difference between a fixed and variable cost?

2 Identify **two** types of decisions that use cost data to help a business.

3 Identify **two** diseconomies of scale.

4 What is the margin of safety?

Sample questions

Dane plans to set up a shoe repair business. His fixed costs are $120 per month and variable costs are $4. The average price of each repair is $5. Based on his market research, Dane expects to get 180 customers per month.

Example 1:
Identify **two** limitations of break-even analysis. **[2]**

Sample answer:
Limitation 1: It assumes that everything made is sold, which is not the case. **[1]**

Limitation 2: Variable costs can fall as output increases, due to economies of scale. **[1]**

Example 2:
Using the information provided, construct a break-even chart for Dane's business. **[4]**

Sample answer:

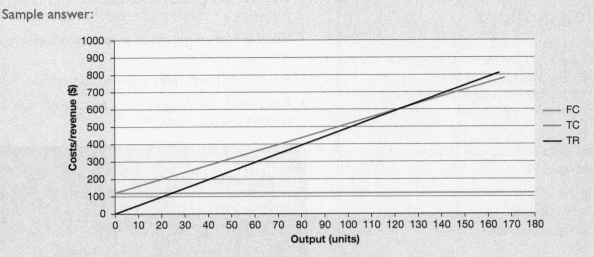

Figure 16.04 A break-even chart for Dane's business.

Example 3:
Explain **two** ways in which break-even analysis might be useful to Dane's business. [6]

Sample answer:
Way 1: It shows the margin of safety [1] so Dane knows that as long as he gets over 120 customers [1], he will make a profit [1].

Way 2: It can help with planning [1] as Dane can estimate how many repairs he needs to do [1], and then can order the right amount of materials [1].

Examination-style questions

AFC makes a wide range of animal feeds for horses and chickens. The products are sold in many countries. AFC benefits from economies of scale. The Operations manager has been looking at some cost and revenue data. She cannot decide whether she should stop production of product B.

	Product A	Product B
Fixed costs per month	$60 000	$45 000
Variable costs per kilo	$4	$3
Average price per kilo	$6	$6
Planned sales per month (kilo)	80 000	30 000

Table 16.03 Cost and revenue data for products.

a   Define 'fixed costs'. [2]

b   Calculate:
   i   the break-even output for product B
   ii profit if the business makes the planned sales of 30 000 per month. [4]

c   Do you think AFC should stop production of product B? Justify your answer. [6]

d   Explain **two** possible economies of scale AFC could benefit from.
   Economy of scale 1:
   Economy of scale 2: [8]

Achieving quality production

Learning summary

By the end of this unit you should understand:

- [ ] why quality is important
- [ ] the concept of quality control and how it can be implemented
- [ ] the concept of quality assurance.

17.01 What quality means

The quality of a product must match what customers expect and the image the business wants to convey. Quality is important for all businesses as it:

- ensures customer satisfaction and builds loyalty
- helps to build and maintain the brand image
- improves the business's reputation
- can lead to increased sales
- can allow the business to charge a higher price
- allows the business to be more competitive
- leads to fewer customer complaints.

17.02 Concept of quality control

Finished products must be checked to make sure that they meet a minimum standard. Poor quality could lead to repair costs, as well as damaging the business's reputation.

How businesses implement quality control

A trained employee (inspector) tests every finished product or samples from each batch. Any faulty items will be discarded or sent for repair. This takes time and money. As this check is made at the end of the process, mistakes made during production could mean many faulty products.

TERMS

Quality control: checking products at the end of the production process to see if they meet the set standard.

Quality assurance: this means checking that standards are being met throughout the production process.

Quality circles: groups of employees from many departments meet regularly to discuss ways to improve quality.

Total quality management (TQM): an approach where everyone in the business is responsible for quality.

17.03 Concept of quality assurance

This is a process where all employees are encouraged to check what they do all the time. This should:

- prevent mistakes from happening
- lower unit costs as there is less wastage of resources at an early stage
- improve motivation as employees are involved in the process.

However, there are a few drawbacks:

- It is a slow process which requires all employees to accept the same approach.
- Employees might need a lot of training and support to adapt to this approach.

Total quality management (TQM) creates a culture of quality. All employees are encouraged to think about customer needs all the time. Everyone tries to get it right first time. TQM is linked to Kaizen and makes use of quality circles, in which groups of employees discuss the quality of the product.

TIP

Quality assurance is about avoiding mistakes. Quality control checks what has been done.

Sample question

SDB makes plastic toys including dolls and cars, using batch production. Following a number of customer complaints, the Operations manager cannot decide whether to introduce quality control or quality assurance.

With reference to SDB, outline the difference between quality control and quality assurance. [4]

Sample answer:
Quality control only happens at the end of the process [1] after toys have been made [1]. Quality assurance takes place throughout production, by employees who can stop mistakes from happening [1] and prevent a lot of materials being wasted [1].

TIP

Remember: there are other ways in which a business can try to improve quality.

Summary

Quality is important for all businesses. Ensuring quality can help a business maintain its image as well as reducing costs. There are two main approaches. Quality control involves checking the final product, while quality assurance tries to prevent mistakes from happening.

Progress check

1   What does quality mean to you?

2   What is the difference between quality control and quality assurance?

3   Identify **two** problems that poor quality can cause.

4   When does quality assurance happen?

Sample questions

Raj owns a successful restaurant in the city centre. He employs eight cooks in the kitchen and 16 people to serve customers. Last year, revenue increased by $30 000. Raj believes that providing a quality service is important if the restaurant is to remain competitive.

Example 1:
Explain **two** reasons why quality might be important to Raj's business. [6]

Sample answer:
Reason 1: Raj can charge high prices [1] as customers will be willing to pay more for the service [1] that will help the restaurant increase revenue [1].

Reason 2: It will help to maintain the restaurant's image [1] as food served will meet the expected standard [1] and the business will remain competitive [1].

Example 2:
Explain **two** ways in which Raj can try to ensure that the restaurant provides a quality service. [8]

Sample answer:
Way 1: Use quality assurance [1] so that all kitchen and serving workers are responsible for service [1]. If everyone tries to avoid mistakes throughout the process [1], a good service should be the end result [1].

Way 2: Offer training [1] so kitchen staff will know how to prepare ingredients properly [1]. This will ensure that the food served is as described in the menu [1], guaranteeing that customers get exactly what they have ordered [1].

Examination-style questions

JCF makes a range of food including biscuits and cakes, using batch production. The Operations Director is looking to improve quality. One option is to introduce quality control. JCF has 45 employees who are always looking for ways to improve how things are done. Machines often break down. JCF has a high level of inventory. The Operations Director cannot decide whether or not introducing new technology is the best way to increase productivity.

a   Define 'quality control'. [2]

b   Outline **two** problems that poor quality might cause JCF.

Problem 1:

Problem 2: [4]

c   Explain **two** ways JCF could improve quality.

Way 1:

Way 2: [8]

d   Explain how the following **three** ways could help JCF to improve the quality of its products. Which way do you think JCF should use? Justify your answer.

Train employees:

Use quality control:

Buy better quality ingredients:

Conclusion: [12]

Location decisions

Learning summary

By the end of this unit you should understand:

- ■ the main factors affecting location decisions of manufacturing and service businesses

- ■ factors to consider when deciding which country to locate operations in

- ■ role of legal controls on location decisions.

Every business, whether producing goods or services, has to be based somewhere.

18.01 Main factors affecting location decisions for a business

Finding the right location involves identifying which factors are the most important for a particular business.

Access to raw materials and suppliers

Some businesses use a lot of raw materials or bulky resources such as coal. Being close to resources can reduce transport costs.

Close to market

If finished goods are expensive or bulky to move, being close to customers can help reduce transport costs. Services are often located near customers for ease of customer access.

Availability of suitable land

The amount of space needed will vary for each business. Is there space to expand or offer facilities such as parking? Does it convey the right image? How much will it cost to buy or rent? Local taxes and insurance need to be paid as well. Costs will vary by region or country and whether or not it is a city centre site.

Climate can be important for certain products such as farming.

Power and water

Many businesses need access to power and electricity to operate equipment.

Labour

If a business needs specialist employees, it should locate where these skills can be found. A business trying to keep labour costs low might choose an area with high unemployment or low costs.

Transport links and communications

Access to materials and customers is important. For importers, exporters and distribution businesses, good transport links are essential. A wholesaler will want good transport links to ensure that supplies can be moved easily between producers and consumers. All businesses want access to telephone/internet networks.

Location of competitors

Being near competitors can be good or bad. Many similar businesses in an area can lead to suppliers setting up nearby, lowering transport costs. The local workforce have the right skills reducing training costs. However, too much competition could limit demand for the product, reducing sales.

Government influence

Grants and other incentives may be offered to persuade a business to locate in a certain area. This can help to lower costs. A government can also put restrictions on locations (see 18.04).

Personal reasons

Owners or managers might like a particular place. Some might want to locate near their home for family reasons or to reduce travel time.

TERMS

Location: a place where a business is based.

Relocation: when a business moves from one place to another.

18.02 Choosing a location

The location of a business has implications for cost and potential revenue. If the site is not suitable, relocating a factory is very expensive or impractical. Not being near your target market could mean lost sales.

Every business is different. Primary, secondary and tertiary sector organisations provide different types of goods or service. Some need to import and/or export materials or finished products.

TIP
There might not be a perfect location. A business will try to find the best fit.

Choosing a location for a manufacturing business

Factors for a manufacturing business to consider include:

- power and water
- transport links
- access to labour
- access to raw materials and supplies
- availability of suitable land – expansion, facilities, cost
- government influence
- distance to market.

TIP
Manufacturers make products. Suitable land, power, labour and transport could be important factors when deciding where to locate.

Sample question

Kape Foods (KF) makes a range of frozen food products such as vegetables and chips. Its products are sold to shops and supermarkets around the country. Due to increased demand, Kape needs to expand by opening a new distribution centre, away from its factory. This will create 300 new jobs.

Consider which **three** factors you think are the most important to KF when making its location decision. Justify your answer. **[12]**

Sample answer:
Transport is important for a distribution centre. It must be near roads so that food can be easily brought in and out. There is no point in locating the centre in a remote area that lorries cannot access, as this will delay deliveries and damage the business's reputation.

Electricity is needed to to keep the frozen food at the right temperature. If the environment is too hot, the chips will defrost. The food would be ruined and have to be remade.

Government might offer **grants** to help a business set up in certain locations. This could help lower its costs. As Kape is creating 300 jobs, a government might want to encourage KF to set up in their region. As its products are sold around the country, KF could locate in many places, so cost can greatly influence their decision.

TIP
In order to improve your answer, do not just list factors, but explain why each one needs to be considered.

Choosing a location for a service business

Factors for a service business to consider include:

- being close to market
- access to labour
- personal reasons
- transport and communication
- availability of suitable land – parking, image, convenience
- being close to competitors.

TIP

Many services involve direct contact with customers. Being close to customers and competitors might be the most important factors, as well as good access to the business.

TIP

Other factors such as market, transport and communication are also important to consider.

Sample question

Amvita wants to set up a flower shop. She has $800 in savings to use as start-up capital. Amvita cannot decide whether a bank overdraft is the best source of finance to use for working capital.

Outline **two** factors Amvita should consider when deciding where to locate her business. [4]

Sample answer:

Factor 1: Being close to the market so that customers can easily access her shop. [2]

Factor 2: The location of her competitors – she might lose out on flower sales if they are too near. [2]

18.03 Factors to consider when deciding in which country to locate operations

For some businesses, including multinational companies, the question is in which country to locate the business.

The answer depends on the reason behind the decision; for example, is the business trying to reduce costs or expand into new market?

- **Rules and regulations** – each country will have its own rules for taxation and what can be made and sold. Incentives might be available as a government tries to meet its economic objectives.
- **Language barrier** – this has implications for management and control.
- **Culture** – traditions and attitudes vary. What is acceptable in one place might cause offence somewhere else.
- **Tariffs and quotas** – these can restrict what and how much can be imported, and can influence where the business is based.

18.04 Role of legal controls in location decisions

Legal controls influence costs. They also restrict where a business can locate and how it is allowed to operate.

- Planning regulations can restrict where a business can locate.
- Environmental controls affect how a business is allowed to operate, for example, waste disposal, machinery, materials or techniques used.
- Employment controls affect areas such as health and safety, and minimum wages.

Figure 18.01 Factors to consider when deciding on the right country for the business.

Summary

There are many factors that could influence location decisions. A business must consider which factors are important based on its situation.

Progress check

1 Identify **three** location factors that any business will need to consider.

2 State **two** factors that might be important to a retailer.

3 Why is climate an issue for some businesses?

4 Outline **two** ways in which legal controls can influence local decisions.

Sample questions

CSG is based in country P. It makes washing machines. Due to increased labour costs, the Managing Director is looking to relocate its factory to another country. She is not sure how legal controls might affect the location decision.

Example 1:
Identify **two** reasons (other than labour costs) why a business might want to relocate. **[2]**

Sample answer:
Reason 1: access to suitable land. **[1]**

Reason 2: changes to legal controls. **[1]**

Example 2:
Outline **two** factors (other than labour costs) CSG should consider when deciding on which country to operate in. **[4]**

Sample answer:
Factor 1: Cost of land **[1]** as the factory will need a large area **[1]**.

Factor 2: Transport links **[1]** as CSG will need to move parts and the finished machines in and out of the factory **[1]**.

Examination-style questions

KLH owns a chain of 40 hotels in different countries. 70% of its guests are business people. KLH has a good reputation and offers competitive prices. The Marketing Director is looking at ways to increase the level of sales. She has a marketing budget of $3m. She said, 'Technology has changed our business. Having a website is very helpful – and not just for advertising and promotion.' KLH has plans to open ten more hotels in the next two years. KLH's Directors know finding the right locations will be important.

a Identify **two** ways a government might influence the location of a business.
Way 1:
Way 2: [2]

b Outline **two** reasons why the right location could be important to KLH.
Reason 1
Reason 2: [4]

c Do you think the right location is the most important factor to the success of KLH's business? Justify your answer. [6]

d Explain why the following **three** factors are important for KLH when deciding on a new location. Which factor do you think is most important? Justify your answer.
Land:
Labour:
Competitors:
Conclusion: [12]

Section 5:
FINANCIAL INFORMATION AND DECISIONS

Business finance: needs and sources

Learning summary

By the end of this unit you should understand:

- ☐ the reasons why businesses need finance

- ☐ the sources of internal and external finance

- ☐ the difference between short-term and long-term finance

- ☐ the difference between loans and shares

- ☐ the factors which affect the method of finance chosen.

19.01 The need for business finance

Every business needs finance. The five main reasons are:

1 Pay start-up costs for a new business, for example, premises, market research, equipment.

2 Finance operations before sales are made, for example, buy materials to make products.

3 Cash to cover day-to-day running costs, for example, pay suppliers for materials.

4 Some customers do not pay for goods immediately. Finance is needed to pay other costs to avoid cash flow problems.

5 To finance expansion or replace old machinery.

Some finance is needed for the short term. This is usually for working capital or operational needs. It is repayable within a year. Long-term finance is generally used for capital expenditure, and is paid back over many years.

TERMS

Capital expenditure: money spent on non-current assets that are expected to last longer than a year.

External finance: money from sources outside the business.

Internal finance: money from sources within the business itself.

Long-term finance: any debts or loans repayable after 12 months.

TERMS

Short-term finance: any debts or loans repayable within 12 months.

Start-up capital: money needed by a business to purchase assets before it can start trading.

19.02 The main sources of finance

Different sources of finance can be classified by the time period in which they need to be repaid. Sources can also be classified by whether the finance has come from inside or outside of the business.

	Internal	External
Short term	• Manage working capital • Reduce inventory • Ask customers to pay quicker • Pay suppliers more slowly	• Bank overdraft • Trade credit • Debt factoring
Long term	• Profit • Owner's capital • Sell non-current assets	• Bank loans • Debentures • Mortgages • Hire purchase and leasing • Issue shares • Borrow from friends/family

Table 19.01 The main sources of finance.

19.03 Internal sources of finance

These come from the business activities or assets. This is a cheap form of finance, as no repayments are needed. The amount of finance raised is limited to how successful the business is or has been.

Manage working capital

This involves making the best use of current assets. It could mean:

- asking customers to pay more quickly
- reducing the amount of inventory held
- taking longer to pay suppliers for materials.

Advantages	Disadvantages
• No interest has to be paid	• Could upset customers if the business asks for quicker payments, so lose sales
• No need to repay	• Not enough inventory to make products
• Can help improve business efficiency	• Suppliers might not provide inventory if the business pays too slowly, or might not provide discounts.

Table 19.02 Advantages and disadvantages of managing working capital.

Sell non-current assets

Any unwanted machinery or land can be sold to raise finance.

Advantages	Disadvantages
• No interest has to be paid	• Can take time to sell assets
• No need to repay	• Might not raise much money
• Better use of resources rather than keeping old assets	• Limited number of assets can be sold

Table 19.03 Advantages and disadvantages of selling non-current assets.

Retained profits/reserves

This is money left over from profit made in previous years that can be put back into the business.

Advantages	Disadvantages
• No interest has to be paid	• Takes time to raise funds
• No need to repay	• Might not raise enough money
• Flexible – use as required	• Opportunity cost – once used, it is not available for other uses

Table 19.04 Advantages and disadvantages of using retained profits/reserves.

Owners' capital or savings

This means using money put into the business by the owners at start-up. This acts as the main source of finance for sole traders.

Advantages	Disadvantages
• No interest has to be paid	• Risk losing own money
• No need to repay	• Might only raise limited amount

Table 19.05 Advantages and disadvantages of using owners' capital or savings.

19.04 External sources of finance

External finance comes from individuals or organisations outside the business. Generally, it is more expensive than internal finance.

Bank overdraft

An overdraft is a short-term loan. It is mainly used for cash flow problems.

Advantages	Disadvantages
• Flexible	• Finance costs
• Can be quick to arrange	• Security might be asked for

Table 19.06 Advantages and disadvantages of having a bank overdraft.

TIP

An overdraft is a type of bank loan. The difference is time. This is a short-term option.

Trade credit

Suppliers allow a business to buy goods now but pay later. It is a short-term measure that can help cash flow.

Advantages	Disadvantages
• No interest has to be paid	• If payment is late, supplier could stop delivery
• Easy to arrange, as most suppliers offer it	• Loss of discounts will increase cost of sales

Table 19.07 Advantages and disadvantages of using trade credit.

Debt factoring

The business sells its outstanding trade receivables to another business in exchange for immediate but not full cash payment.

Advantages	Disadvantages
• Quick access to cash	• Do not receive full amount of debt owed
• Not responsible for collecting debts owed	

Table 19.08 Advantages and disadvantages of debt factoring.

Leasing

The business pays a set monthly amount to use or rent machinery, building or land.

Advantages	Disadvantages
• No large initial payment needed	• The business never owns the asset, so cannot sell it if needed
• Lease company may cover cost of repair	• Overall cost will be higher due to high monthly payments
• Can update or replace if and when technology improves	

Table 19.09 Advantages and disadvantages of leasing.

Hire purchase

A business buys an asset in fixed amounts while having the benefit of using it before full payment is made.

Advantages	Disadvantages
• No large initial payment needed	• Responsible for maintenance
• The business owns item at end of agreement	• Monthly payments must be made. Total cost can be higher than buying item

Table 19.10 Advantages and disadvantages of hire purchase.

TIP A key difference between hire purchase and lease is what happens to the asset at the end. Hire purchase is owned by the business. Lease items are returned.

Bank loan

A bank loan is repayable after 12 months. These are mainly for used for capital expenditure.

Advantages	Disadvantages
• The business has a set time period to repay	• Finance costs
• Large amounts of money can be borrowed	• Security needed if the business cannot repay
• No risk to ownership (unlike shares)	• Increases risk as interest must be paid, whether or not the business makes a profit. Lender can force business to sell assets to repay them, or even close down the business

Table 19.11 Advantages and disadvantages of having a bank loan.

Mortgage

This is used specifically to purchase land or buildings. The asset itself acts as security in case the loan cannot be repaid.

Debenture

Limited companies can issue a bond to raise large sums of money. Lenders receive a fixed rate of interest each year.

Issue shares (equity)

Limited companies can issue shares to shareholders to raise large sums of money. Mainly used for capital expenditure.

TIP A business does NOT have to pay a dividend (it is optional), unlike interest on loans.

Advantages	Disadvantages
• No need to repay	• Risk of takeover if too many shares are issued
• No interest payable (dividends are paid only if the business is successful)	• Only an option for limited companies
	• Less control for existing shareholders

Table 19.12 Advantages and disadvantages of issuing shares.

Borrow from friends/family

Many sole traders and small businesses might ask people they know for finance.

Advantages	Disadvantages
• No interest or security needed	• Only likely to raise small amounts
• Possibly quicker than asking the bank for finance	• Time period and conditions for borrowing money unsure

Table 19.13 Advantages and disadvantages of borrowing from friends/family.

TERMS

Overdraft: an amount of money borrowed from a bank that is repayable within 12 months.

Trade credit: an arrangement to buy goods or services from suppliers without having to make an immediate cash payment.

Bank loan: finance provided by a bank which is repayable after 12 months.

19.05 Alternative sources of capital

Micro-finance

In some countries, entrepreneurs do not have access to traditional sources of finance. With no savings or people to support them, their businesses are seen as too high a risk. Micro-finance is used in this instance.

TERM

Micro-finance: financial services, including small loans, provided to poor people who are not served by traditional banks.

TIP

When explaining why a method is suitable, avoid using simple statements such as 'it's cheaper'. Try to explain how or why it might be cheaper.

Sample question

Lara is a sole trader. She has a successful small taxi business. Lara wants to expand by offering an airport taxi service to and from the city. Lara needs to buy an eight-seater vehicle to carry people and their luggage. It will cost $9000. She has few savings as she has invested everything into the business. Her current overdraft is $1500. She thinks she has three options – increase her overdraft, bank loan or lease a vehicle.

State the advantages and disadvantages of the following **three** sources of finance Lara could use:
• bank overdraft
• bank loan
• leasing

Which source of finance do you think Lara should use? Justify your answer. [12]

Sample answer:
Bank overdraft: Overdraft is not appropriate for capital expenditure as Lara needs $9000. An overdraft is also only for up to one year. It could take much longer for Lara to repay such a large amount.

If she cannot pay it back, she risks losing her business and personal belongings, as she is a sole trader.

Bank loan: Lara could raise the full amount and repay the $9000 slowly over a number of years. This would allow time to generate revenue from the new service to pay off the loan. However she will have to pay interest, which will increase her costs.

Leasing: Lara pays a set amount each month to use the vehicle. If the taxi breaks down, Lara might not have to pay anything, saving money on repairs. The only problem is she will not own it so cannot count it as a non-current asset. It could cost more each month to lease it if the leasing company charges a lot, so overall she might end up spending more on the vehicle and have nothing to show for it at the end of the lease.

Conclusion: Leasing is the best option for Lara. She can upgrade it to a new model whenever she wants which might help attract and keep customers. If the airport service does not work, she can return it so this can reduce the risk. With a loan she could still be paying for the vehicle even when it is no longer useful.

Crowd-funding is another alternative source of capital.

TERM

Crowd-funding: financing a business idea by obtaining small amounts of capital from a large number of people, most often using the internet and social media networks.

19.06 Main factors considered in making financial choices

Why, when, who, how long and how much are the key factors that will influence the choice of finance selected. Deciding on the best option depends on the situation. Not all options are available to all businesses.

Progress check

1 List **three** different types of capital a business might need.

2 What does the word 'internal' mean in terms of finance?

3 What is the difference between a loan and a share?

4 State **one** use of long-term finance for a limited company.

Summary

Businesses need money for many reasons. There are many sources of finance available. There are many factors which can be used to help decide on what is an appropriate source(s) in given circumstances.

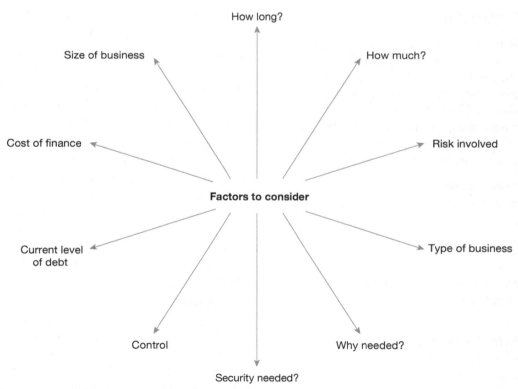

Figure 19.01 Factors to consider when making financial choices.

Sample questions

Amvita wants to start up a flower shop. She has $800 in savings to use as start-up capital. Amvita cannot decide whether a bank overdraft is the best source of finance to use for working capital.

Example 1:
Define 'bank overdraft'. [2]

Sample answer:
This is an amount of money borrowed from the bank [1] that is repayable within 12 months [1].

Example 2:
Identify **two** possible start-up costs that Amvita might have. [2]

Sample answer:
Cost 1: Shop. [1]

Cost 2: Tables for displaying flowers. [1]

Example 3:
Outline **two** factors Amvita should consider when choosing a source of finance. [4]

Sample answer:
Factor 1: Cost, as she will have to pay interest on loan. [2]

Factor 2: Purpose, as it is for working capital, so short-term methods should be used. [2]

Examination-style questions

YPEE is a private limited company. It makes pottery, including plates and cups. Last year profits fell to $1m. The Finance Director wants to raise $5m to introduce new technology into the production process. He said 'There are so many sources of finance including leasing to choose from.' He cannot decide whether debt is a better option than issuing shares to raise the finance. YPEE does not have any non-current assets to sell.

a   Identify **one** advantage and **one** disadvantage of selling non-current assets.
Advantage:
Disadvantage: [2]

b   Outline **two** factors YPEE should consider when deciding on a source of finance.
Factor 1:
Factor 2:   [4]

c   Do you think it is better for YPEE to use debt rather than issue shares? Justify your answer.   [6]

d   State the advantages and disadvantages of the following **three** sources of finance YPEE could use. Which source of finance do you think it should use? Justify your answer.
Profit:
Leasing:
Issue shares:
Conclusion: [12]

Cash flow forecasting and working capital

20.01 Why cash is important to a business

Every business needs money, so managing cash is important. Without enough cash, even a profitable business will fail. Timing is key – when does money enter and need to leave the business? A business must have access to money at the right time to ensure that it can pay day-to-day expenses. If it cannot, the following scenarios could occur:

- Suppliers could stop supplying materials or offering discounts. Delays can impact on production and productivity.

- Unfulfilled orders can lead to customer complaints, damaging the business's reputation.

- Unpaid workers could become demotivated.

- Lenders might charge higher interest rates on loans, as the business is seen as higher risk.

20.02 The cash flow forecast and its importance

A business needs to know it will have enough cash to operate. A cash flow forecast is a tool to help a business manage its money by anticipating problems. A cash flow forecast:

- can predict gaps and shortfalls between cash in and out

- gives the business time to arrange extra funds if needed to cover any shortfalls

- helps loan applications, as it can show why the money is needed, and demonstrate the business's ability to repay in future

- helps business planning.

If cash outflows are more than cash inflows, there will be a shortfall (negative cash flow). The business may not be able to pay debts due straightaway.

TERM

Cash flow forecast: this shows the estimated amount of money coming into and going out of a business over a period of time, usually one year.

Worked example

Gr8Gear is a retail shop in the city centre. It sells a range of ladies' clothes. The manager, Ling, is worried about cash flow. She has constructed a cash flow forecast for the next three months.

	Month 1	Month 2	Month 3
Cash inflows			
Cash sales	550	580	600
Total cash inflow (a)	550	580	600
Cash outflows			
Inventory	220	220	200
Rent	**300**	**0**	**0**
Other costs	280	260	260
Total cash outflow (b)	800	480	460
Net cash flow (c) = (a) − (b)	(250)	100	140
Opening balance (d)	(30)	(280)	(180)
Closing balance (c) + (d)	(280)	(180)	(40)

Table 20.01 Gr8Gear cash flow (amounts in $).

What does this show?

A negative cash flow is expected in all three months. This is due to the rent payment in month 1.

Note: Revenue is included only when the money is received. This may not be when goods were sold, as customers might buy goods on credit.

TERMS

Cash flow: flow of all money in and out of the business.

Cash inflows: money coming into the business. This includes cash from sales, proceeds from sale of assets and money from loans and grants.

Cash outflows: money going out of the business. This includes wages, rent, material costs, advertising and interest payments.

Net cash flow: the difference between cash inflows and outflows over the period.

Closing balance: the amount of cash left at the end of the period.

Opening balance: the amount of cash at the beginning of the period.

Sample question

Outline how a cash flow forecast might help Gr8Gear. [4]

Sample answer:
This can show Ling when and how much cash is needed to pay all her bills, such as rent which is due for review in March. If she knows when she might have a problem, she can ask for help before she needs it. Banks are more likely to give her a $300 overdraft, as she has shown that she can repay it over the next few months. [4]

20.03 Ways to solve cash flow problems

The right solution will often depend on the reason. Solutions can include:

- increase cash sales
- short-term loan
- arrange a bank overdraft
- reduce amount of inventory held
- ask trade receivables to pay more quickly
- ask trade payables for more time
- use trade credit.

Worked example

For Gr8Gear, the problem is the rent. If rent is paid over 12 months, a negative cash flow is expected in month 1. Cash flow is positive in months 2 and 3.

	Month 1	Month 2	Month 3
Total cash inflow (a)	550	580	600
Cash out			
Inventory	220	220	200
Rent	25	25	25
Other costs	280	260	260
Total cash outflow (b)	525	505	485
Net cash flow (c) = (a) − (b)	25	75	115
Opening balance (d)	(30)	(5)	70
Closing balance (c) + (d)	(5)	70	185

Table 20.02 Gr8Gear cash flow (amounts in $).

TIP

You can be asked to complete a simple cash flow forecast, so make sure you know where the numbers should be.

20.04 The concept of working capital

A business is solvent ('liquid') if it can meet its short-term debts when they need to be paid.

Working capital is more than cash; for example, if the inventory is too high, cash is tied up.

Working capital is needed to:

• pay wages and trade payables

• buy inventory to produce goods

• be able to offer and receive discounts.

Working capital = Current assets − Current liabilities

Figure 20.01 How to calculate working capital.

The amount of working capital needed will vary, depending on the product and type of business.

TERMS

Liquidity: the ability of a firm to meet its short-term debts.

Working capital: money to cover day-to-day running costs.

Sample question

Amvita wants to start up a flower shop. She has $800 in savings to use as start-up capital. Amvita cannot decide whether a bank overdraft is the best source of finance to use for working capital.

Define 'working capital'. [2]

Sample answer:
Working capital shows how many liquid assets a business has to finance its everyday costs. [2]

Progress check

1 Identify **one** reason why a business might need cash.

2 What is the purpose of a cash flow forecast?

3 Identify **two** cash outflows that a small business might have.

4 Why is working capital not the same as cash?

Summary

Cash is important to a business, and many businesses use a cash flow forecast to help avoid or solve financial problems. Working capital is a way to measure liquidity, to check whether a business can pay its short-term debts.

Sample questions

STH makes a range of luxury boats. The owner Gee is always worried about cash flow. He said, 'I pay all suppliers in 30 days. But it takes me six months to be paid by customers. Just look at my cash flow forecast – I need to do something.'

	Month 1	Month 2	Month 3
Cash inflows	20	80	40
Cash outflows	30	40	30
Net cash flow	(10)	40	Y
Opening balance	(20)	X	0
Closing balance	(30)	0	10

Table 20.03 Cash flow forecast for STH ($000s).

Example 1:
Define 'cash flow forecast'. [2]

Sample answer:
A cash flow forecast shows the amount of money going in and out of a business [1] over a period of time [1].

Example 2:
Calculate the values for X and Y. [2]

Sample answer:
X: (30) [1]

Y: 10 [1]

Example 3:
Outline **two** possible ways STH could improve its cash flow. [4]

Sample answer:
Way 1: ask customers to pay more quickly [1] so the business receives cash earlier than six months [1].

Way 2: arrange an overdraft [1] so STH can pay suppliers in 30 days [1].

Examination-style questions

Sylvia owns a market stall selling local fruits and vegetables. Sales have fallen since a new supermarket opened nearby. Sylvia is worried about cash flow. She said, 'The supermarket can offer low prices and more products. I have to throw away a lot of food that I have paid for. Suppliers want to be paid when I buy. Should I start customer credit terms? ' Sylvia has produced a cash flow forecast.

	January	February	March
Cash inflows	800	770	750
Cash out:			
Bought fruit/veg	450	450	550
Other costs including wages	280	280	300
Net cash flow	70	Y	(100)
Opening balance	0	70	110
Closing balance	X	110	10

Table 20.04 Cash flow forecast for Sylvia (in $).

a   Define 'closing balance'? [2]

b   Calculate the values for:
X:
Y: [2]

c   Explain **two** possible reasons why Sylvia might have cash flow problems.
Reason 1:
Reason 2: [6]

d   Explain **two** ways Sylvia could improve her cash flow position. Recommend which way she should use.
Justify your answer. [6]

Income statements

21.01 What is profit, and why it is important?

Profit is the difference between revenue and total costs. It is a key objective for private sector businesses. Why? Profit is:

- the reward for risk-taking

- a measure of success

- a source of internal finance for reinvestment

- needed for long-term survival of the business.

TERMS

Profit: what is left over from revenue after all costs have been paid, **or** total revenue minus total cost.

Revenue: the income of the business from sale of products in a period of time, **or** price multiplied by quantity sold.

21.02 The difference between cash and profit

Profit is not the same as cash. Profit is the surplus of revenue after all costs have been paid. Cash is money that is immediately available to spend.

The difference is timing. Profit is recorded when the sale is made, and cash flow is recorded when the money is actually received.

TIP

Profit matters in the long term. Cash is more important in the short term.

Worked example

CarKit makes car components. It buys materials from its supplier on 40 days' credit. It sells the finished components to other businesses. CarKit allows customers 60 days to pay. The Managing Director plans to spend $50 000 on a new machine so that it can increase production. How does this affect profit and cash?

	Impact on profit	Impact on cash flow
Customer buys $10 000 worth of goods on 60 days' credit	$10 000 increase in revenue now	No change until customer payment received
Materials costing $6000 bought on 40 days' credit	$6000 increase in cost of sales now	Cash outflow recorded when the business pays for the materials (40 days later)
Buy new machine for $50 000	No impact: non-current assets are listed in statement of financial position	Cash outflow of $50 000 when the business pays for the machine

Table 21.01 Impacts on profit and cash flow.

Sample question

Outline **two** reasons why profit might be important for CarKit. **[4]**

Sample answer:
Reason 1: It is a sign of success, so customers might be more willing to buy components from them. **[2]**

Reason 2: It is a source of finance that can be used to purchase the new machine. **[2]**

21.03 The main features of an income statement

An income statement shows whether or not the business has made a profit. It is useful so that the business can:

- see its performance during a given period
- compare performance with other years or businesses
- plan, as it can see how decisions might impact on revenue or costs.

TERMS

Income statement: this statement records the income and expenditure of a business over a given period of time.

Cost of sales: the variable costs of making a product. This includes the cost of materials and direct labour.

Gross profit: this is calculated by revenue minus cost of sales.

Expenses: costs not directly linked to producing the product, for example rent, insurance, marketing.

Tax: the amount of tax on business profit which is payable to the government.

Dividend: the share of profit given to shareholders.

Retained profit: the amount of profit kept which can be reinvested back into the business.

21.04 The layout of an income statement

Worked example

Z Foods owns a chain of 300 supermarkets.

	December 2016 ($m)	December 2015 ($m)
Total revenue	180	120
Less cost of sales	(90)	(60)
Gross profit	90	60
Less expenses	(60)	(45)
Profit (before tax)	30	15
Less tax	(10)	(5)
Profit after tax	20	10
Dividends	(5)	(2)
Retained profit	15	8

Table 21.02 Income statement for Z Foods for period years ending 2016 and 2015.

TIP You will not be asked to construct an income statement, but you may need to complete missing figures. Learn which figures to add or subtract to work out each value.

Use of simple income statements in decision-making based on profit calculations

Using the worked example of Z Foods, many simple observations can be made about profit:

- gross profit increased by $30m to $90m
- profit increased by $10 to $20m
- retained profit increased by $7m to $15m.

This shows that:

- Profit has increased, which suggests an improved performance.
- Gross profit increased by $30m, but retained profit only increased by $7m.
- Z Foods may want to reduce its expenses to ensure that maximum profit is made.

Sample question

Paolo has a takeaway curry shop. He wants to know how much profit he makes each week.

Selling price per curry	$6
Cost of sales	$3
Expenses per week	$2400
Average sales per week	1200

Table 21.03 Sales and cost information for Paolo's business ($).

Calculate how much profit Paolo makes in one week. [4]

Sample answer:

Total revenue =   6 × 1200   = $7200

Total cost =   (3 × 1200) + 2400   = $6000

Profit   = $1200

Progress check

1   What is profit?

2   What does an income statement show?

3   What is included in cost of sales?

4   What is the difference between gross profit and profit?

Summary

Profit is an important objective for many businesses. An income statement shows the profit (or loss) made by a business by subtracting the costs from the revenue made.

Sample questions

Tickers makes watches and clocks. Each clock sells for $200.

Revenue	X
Cost of sales	180
Gross profit	120
Expenses	Y
Profit	30

Table 21.04 Tickers' income statement for year ending 31 December 2016 ($000).

Example 1:
Calculate the values of X and Y. [2]

Sample answer:
X: $300 000 [1]

Y: $90 000 [1]

TIP Always check that you have the right number of zeros.

Example 2:
As Tickers has $30 000 in profit, the owner thinks he should have the same amount of cash. Outline why this might not be the case. [4]

Sample answer:
Profit is not the same as cash. Tickers could actually have no cash in the bank because a clock could have been sold to someone who has not paid yet. This is recorded as $200 in sales, so will count towards profit. But it is not cash until Tickers receives the money.

Examination-style questions

Shakers owns 60 bookshops. It is a competitive market. The Managing Director has two objectives – expansion and improving profits. She thinks the best way to achieve this is to increase the number of customers. She said, 'I want to create a website to sell books and open more shops.' In 2015, profits were $8m.

Revenue	30
Cost of sales	(18)
Gross profit	X
Expenses	(6)
Profit	6
Tax	(2)
Retained profit	Y

Table 21.05 Income statement for year ending 31 December 2016 ($m).

a   Define 'revenue'. [2]

b   Calculate the values for:
X:
Y: [2]

c   Explain **two** possible problems for Shakers of a decrease in profit.
Problem 1:
Problem 2: [6]

d   Explain **two** ways (other than increasing the number of customers) Shakers could use to improve its profits.
Way 1:
Way 2: [8]

Statement of financial position

Learning summary

By the end of this unit you should understand:

- the main elements of a statement of financial position
- how to interpret a simple statement of financial position, and make deductions from it.

22.01 Main elements of a statement of financial position

Where does a business get its money from, and what does it do with it?

Assets		Liabilities
Items owned by business Non-current assets + current assets	=	Payments business owes to others Current and non-current liabilities, share capital, retained profit

Figure 22.01 Assets and liabilities.

TERMS

Statement of financial position: shows the value of assets and liabilities of a business at a particular point in time.

Non-current assets: items owned which are expected to last more than a year.

Current assets: short-term assets which will last less than a year.

Inventory: materials, work-in-progress and finished items not yet sold.

Trade receivables: money owed to a business by customers who have bought items on credit.

Trade payables: amount a business owes to its suppliers for goods bought on credit.

Cash: money held in the bank or by the business.

Current liabilities: money owed which has to be paid back in less than one year.

Non-current liabilities: money owed which has to be paid back after one year.

TIP

Inventory is the least liquid **current asset**, as it is not as easy to sell for **cash**.

The first part of the statement of financial position shows what the business owns. The second part of the statement shows how net assets were financed.

Assets		**($000)**
Non-current assets		120
Current assets		
Inventory	45	
Trade receivables	30	
Cash	15	
	90	
Less Current liabilities		
Trade payables	60	
Net current assets	30	
Net assets		**150**
Financed by:		
Shareholders' equity:		
Capital		60
Retained profit/reserves		50
Non-current liabilities		40
Capital employed		**150**

Figure 22.02 Z Foods statement of financial position as at 31 December 2016.

Net assets – what business has done with its money

Non-current assets
for example, land, buildings, machinery

+

Current assets
for example, inventory, trade receivables and cash

–

Less current liabilities
for example, bank overdraft and trade payables

=

Capital employed – where the money came from

Owners' or shareholders' equity

+

Retained profit and reserves

+

Non-current liabilities
for example, bank loans, mortgages

Figure 22.03 How a statement of financial position works

TERMS

Net current assets: current assets less current liabilities (the same as working capital).

Net assets: net value of all assets owned by the business, **or** fixed assets plus net current assets.

Owners' or shareholders' equity:* total amount owed by the business to owners.

Share capital:* money put into the business when shares were originally issued.

Capital employed: total of all long-term and permanent capital of a business.

*Note: only limited companies have shareholders.

TIP

Although you won't be required to create a statement of financial position yourself, remember to revise simple calculations and learn where each item belongs and what it shows in one which may be provided.

Sample question

FAL is a successful transport delivery company. It plans to expand by offering more services to its business customers. The Finance Director has been looking at its statement of financial position.

Define 'statement of financial position'.

Sample answer:
A statement of financial position shows the value of assets and liabilities of a business at a particular point in time.

22.02 How to interpret a simple statement of financial position and make deductions

Stakeholders are interested in the statement of financial position to:

- see what the business is worth, and how this has been financed

- assess liquidity by calculating ratios.

Sample question

FAL is a successful transport delivery company. It plans to expand by offering more services to its business customers. The Finance Director has been looking at its statement of financial position. An extract is shown in Table 22.01.

	As at 30 Jan 2016 ($m)	As at 30 Jan 2017 ($m)
Non-current assets	75	90
Current assets	30	45
Current liabilities	20	30
Non-current liabilities	20	25
Shareholders' equity	65	80

Table 22.01 Extract from FAL's statement of financial position.

Explain **two** possible reasons why shareholders' equity might have increased. [8]

Sample answer

Reason 1: More profit was made in 2016. The business had a successful year, so an extra $15m was kept as retained profit which can be used to help expansion. [4]

Reason 2: There was an increase in share capital. Shareholders bought new shares as the business looked to expand its transport business. Share capital can be used as a source of finance to provide the new services. [4]

Progress check

1. What does the term 'current liability' include?
2. Identify **two** examples of non-current assets.
3. What should capital employed balance with?
4. What time period does a statement of financial position cover?

Summary

The statement of financial position shows what the business owns, owes and how it is financed.

Sample questions

Shoof is a shoe retailer. Table 22.02 is an extract from its statement of financial position as at 28 February 2016.

Non-current assets	200 000
Current assets	884 000
Current liabilities	680 000
Net assets	?

Table 22.02 Extract from Shoof's statement of financial position.

Example 1:
Define 'non-current assets'. [2]

Sample answer:
This means items owned by a business [1] which are expected to last for more than a year [1].

Example 2:
Calculate the value of Shoof's net assets [2].

Sample answer:
Net assets = non-current assets + (current assets – current liabilities)

= 200 000 + 204 000 = 404 000 [2]

Examination-style questions

TAC is a public limited company. It makes metal cutlery including forks and spoons. Due to increased demand, TAC is looking to increase production. An extract of TAC's statement of financial position is shown in Table 22.03.

	As at 31/12/16 ($m)	As at 31/12/15 ($m)
Non-current assets	70	60
Current assets	40	20
Current liabilities	10	20
Shareholders' equity	50	40
Non-current liabilities	50	20

Table 22.03 Extract of TAC's statement of financial position.

a Define 'current assets'. [2]

b Identify **two** examples of current liabilities TAC might have. [2]
Example 1:
Example 2:

c Explain **two** possible reasons for the changes shown in the statement of financial position.
Reason 1:
Reason 2: [6]

d Explain **two** ways stakeholders could use the statement of financial position information.
Way 1:
Way 2: [8]

Analysis of accounts

23.01 How to interpret financial statements

Ratios allow a business to look at its financial performance. This allows a business to:

- judge business results
- identify trends in performance over time
- make comparisons with similar companies
- make decisions.

TIP The ratios covered in the syllabus focus on profitability and liquidity.

23.02 Profitability ratios

Profitability measures how much profit a business makes. As profit is a key objective for a private sector business, stakeholders want each ratio to increase.

Gross profit margin

This shows how much profit a business makes after allowing for cost of sales.

The formula for calculating gross profit margin is:

$$\frac{\text{Gross profit}}{\text{Revenue}} \times 100 = \%$$

Worked example

For Z Foods in 2016, gross profit was $90m, revenue was $150m.

To calculate the gross profit margin:

$$\frac{90}{150} \times 100 = \textbf{60 \%}$$

What does this mean? It shows the business made 60 cents in gross profit for every dollar of revenue in 2016.

Is this good? You would need to compare the result with 2015 to see if this has improved or not:

2015 data:

Gross profit margin = 60/120 × 100 = 50%

2016 vs 2015: the ratio has improved indicating the margin has increased.

There are two ways to improve gross profit margin:

- increase revenue (sell more or increase prices) but maintain cost of sales
- cut cost of sales by lowering wages or material costs.

TIP Always remember to include the formula for ratios used. Check that you have used the figures for the right year.

Profit margin

This is used to show how well expenses are controlled.

> **TIP**
> The **profit margin** will be lower than **gross profit margin** as all costs are included.

The formula for calculating the profit margin is:

$$\frac{\text{Profit}}{\text{Revenue}} \times 100 = \%$$

Worked example

For Z Foods in 2016, profit was $30m, while revenue was $180m

$$\frac{30}{180} \times 100 = \textbf{16.6\%}$$

This shows that the business made 16.6 cents profit for every dollar of revenue in 2016.

Is this good? You would need to compare the result with 2015 to see if this has improved or not:

2015 data:

Profit margin = 15/150 × 100 = 10%

2016 vs 2015: the ratio has improved. Expenses are better controlled.

There are two ways to improve profit margin:

- increase revenue more than expenses
- reduce expenses while maintaining level of sales.

> **TERMS**
>
> Gross profit margin: the amount of gross profit made for every dollar of revenue.
>
> Profit margin: the amount of profit made for every dollar of revenue after expenses.
>
> Return on capital employed (ROCE): this measures how efficiently a business uses its capital to make a profit.

23.03 Return on capital employed (ROCE)

This formula measures the amount of profit made for each dollar invested. The ratio is helpful to investors and managers as its shows how efficiently capital is used.

The formula used to calculate ROCE is:

$$\frac{\text{Profit}}{\text{Capital employed}} \times 100 = \%$$

Worked example

For Z Foods in 2016, profit was $30m, while capital employed was $150m.

$$\frac{30}{150} \times 100 = \textbf{20\%}$$

What does this mean? It shows that the business made 20 cents profit for every dollar invested in 2016.

Is this good? You would need to compare the result with 2015 to see if this has improved or not:

2015 data:

ROCE = 15/120 × 100 = 12.5%

2016 vs 2015: the ratio has improved, which shows that the business used resources better to generate profit.

There are two ways to improve ROCE:

- make better use of capital employed without reducing profit
- increase profit with the same amount of capital employed.

> **TIP**
> You only need to make simple comments about what the ratios show.

Sample questions

Tickers makes watches and clocks. Each clock sells for $200.

Revenue	300
Cost of sales	180
Gross profit	120
Expenses	90
Profit	30

Table 23.01 Extract from Tickers' income statement for year ending 31 December 2016 (in $000).

Example 1:
Calculate the gross profit margin. **[2]**

Sample answer:
$$120/300 \times 100 = 40\%$$

Example 2:
Calculate the profit margin. **[2]**

Sample answer:
$$30/300 \times 100 = 10\%$$

Liquidity ratios

Lenders and suppliers want to know that a business can pay its short-term debts. A low value for either ratio could indicate cash flow problems. Too high, and the business may not be using resources effectively.

TIP

There are no 'ideal' liquidity ratios. What is an acceptable level depends on the type of business. Look at the trend over time or between similar businesses.

Current ratio

This ratio shows whether the business can pay its current liabilities out of current assets.

The formula for calculating the current ratio is:

$$\frac{\text{Current assets}}{\text{Current liabilities}}$$

Worked example

For Z Foods, current assets are $90m, while current liabilities are $60m.

$$\frac{90}{60} = 1.5 \text{ times}$$

The business has 1.5 times the value of current assets for every dollar of current liability.

Is this good? You would need to compare it to previous data.

2015 Data:

$$\frac{75}{60} = 1.25 \text{ times}$$

2016 vs 2015: the ratio has improved, so the business is better able to pay short-term debts.

Acid test ratio

Inventory can be difficult to sell quickly to obtain cash. Ignoring inventory can provide a more realistic view of liquidity.

The formula for calculating acid test ratio is:

$$\frac{\text{Current assets} - \text{inventory}}{\text{Current liabilities}}$$

Worked example

For Z Foods, current assets are $90m, while inventory is $45m. Current liabilities are $60m

$$\frac{90 - 45}{60} = 0.75 \text{ times}$$

This means that the business has 0.75 current assets for every current liability.

You would need to compare this data with the previous year to see if this is an improvement:

2015 Data:

$$\frac{75 - 15}{60} = 1.00 \text{ times}$$

2016 vs 2015: the ratio has decreased, so the business is less able to pay short-term debts unless inventory can be sold.

Acid test ratio: the ability of a business to pay its short-term debts, excluding the value of inventory.

Current ratio: the ability of a business to pay its short-term debts from its current assets.

23.04 Limitations of ratio analysis

Ratios only act as a guide to help decision-making.

- Ratios are based on past results, so cannot predict future.

- To be useful, ratios must be compared to previous years to identify trends, or against similar businesses to assess competitiveness.

- There are many ways to measure asset values. This will affect results.

- Businesses have different liquidity requirements.

- Ratios only consider financial data. Other factors can also affect performance.

23.05 The concept of liquidity

Liquid assets are cash or any assets that can be turned into cash quickly. A business needs to know if it has enough working capital to meet day-to-day running costs.

23.06 How and why accounts are used

Most stakeholders are interested in business performance. Financial statements contain a lot of useful information.

Stakeholder	Why interested	Useful ratios/information
Shareholders	• How well is the business doing?	Profitability ratios
	• Is the value of investment up or down?	Profit figures
	• To decide future investment	Dividend paid
Lenders	• Whether loans will be repaid – how risky is the business?	Profitability ratios
	• Will interest will be repaid on time?	Liquidity ratios
		Cash flow forecast
Trade payables	• How secure is their money?	Profitability ratios
	• Is the business able to repay on time?	Liquidity ratios
Employees	• Level of profit, to decide on possible bonus	Profit figures
	• Job security	Future objectives
Managers	• See how well the business is doing so they can spot problems	Profitability ratios
	• Level of profit influences bonus	Liquidity ratios
	• How secure are their jobs?	Profit figures
		Future objectives
Customers	• Will the business be able to supply goods on time?	Profit figures
		Future objectives
Government	• Profitable businesses are likely to pay more tax	Profit figures
	• How secure are jobs for local community?	Future objectives

Table 23.02 Why financial statements are useful for different stakeholders.

Ratio	Measures	Formula	From
Current	Liquidity	$\dfrac{\text{Current assets}}{\text{Current liabilities}}$	Statement of financial position
Acid test	Liquidity	$\dfrac{\text{Current assets} - \text{inventory}}{\text{Current liabilities}}$	Statement of financial position
Gross profit margin	Performance	$\dfrac{\text{Gross profit}}{\text{Revenue}} \times 100 = \%$	Income statement
Profit margin	Performance	$\dfrac{\text{Profit}}{\text{Revenue}} \times 100 = \%$	Income statement
Return on Capital Employed	Performance	$\dfrac{\text{Profit}}{\text{Capital employed}} \times 100 = \%$	Income statement AND Statement of financial position

Table 23.03 Showing which figures come from which documents.

Progress check

1   Why is ratio analysis used?

2   State **two** liquidity ratios.

3   Write out the formula for Return on Capital Employed.

4   Identify **two** stakeholder groups interested in financial statements.

Summary

There are five ratios to learn. Stakeholders will look at different ratios and information, depending on what they are interested in.

Sample questions

BNH sells a range of luxury cars. The Finance manager is pleased. He said, '2016 has been a successful year. I hope this means 2017 will be good too!' He cannot decide whether or not BNH's liquidity is a problem. Interest rates are expected to fall in 2017.

	2015	2016
Current assets	900	1000
Current liabilities	750	800
Current ratio	1.2	
Acid test ratio	0.9	0.75

Table 23.04 Extract of financial information.

Example 1:
Calculate the current ratio for 2016. [2]

Sample answer:

$$\frac{1000}{800} \text{ [1]} = 1.25 \text{ times [1]}$$

Example 2:
Outline what the results show about BNH's liquidity position. [2]

Sample answer:
Current ratio has improved by 0.5 [1] so the business can pay its short-term debts slightly more easily. [1]

Example 3:
Do you think the Finance manager should be worried by BNH's liquidity position? Justify your answer. [6]

Sample answer:
Current ratio has increased slightly [1] but only by 0.05 [1] so BNH will find it easier to pay its short-term debts [1]. However, acid test has fallen by 0.15 times [1]. This is bad. Even though BNH has been successful, and current ratio has increased, as inventory is the least liquid asset it is not easily converted into cash [1]. The Finance manager should be worried as he could find it difficult to pay short-term debts quickly. [1]

Examination-style questions

HGB makes bicycles. The Finance Director has been looking at some financial information. She thinks 2016 was a successful year as country X has had an economic recession. HGB plans to invest in new machinery next year.

	2015	2016
Revenue ($m)	700	720
Cost of sales ($m)	476	480
Gross profit ($m)	224	240
Expenses ($m)	119	96
Profit ($m)	105	144
ROCE (%)	10%	9%

Table 23.05 Extract of financial information for years ending 2015 and 2016.

a   Calculate the profit margin for 2016.   [2]

b   Outline **two** possible limitations to HGB of using ratio analysis.
Limitation 1:
Limitation 2:   [4]

c   Identify **two** stakeholder groups and explain how each stakeholder group might find HGB's financial statements useful.
Stakeholder 1:
Stakeholder 2:   [8]

d   Refer to the table. Consider the financial information of HGB. Do you think the director should be pleased with HGB's performance? Justify your answer using appropriate ratios.   [12]

Section 6:
EXTERNAL INFLUENCES ON BUSINESS ACTIVITY

Economic issues

Learning summary

By the end of this unit you should understand:

- [ ] government economic objectives

- [ ] the main stages of the business cycle

- [ ] how changes in taxation and interest rates affect business activity, and how businesses might respond to these changes.

24.01 Government economic objectives

Governments influence business activity in order to achieve their economic objectives, which could include the following:

- **Increasing Gross Domestic Product (GDP)** – economic growth means that more goods and services are produced. People enjoy a higher standard of living.

- **Low unemployment** – if people have jobs, they earn money and pay taxes.

- **Low inflation** – this can help to promote economic growth as there is less risk of prices rising too quickly. Businesses want to avoid increased labour and material costs. High prices can lead to lower demand and revenue.

- **Positive balance of payments** – a country will want exports to be higher than imports. This will ensure that more foreign currency enters the economy.

TERMS

Balance of payments: the difference in total value between exports and imports of a country over a year.

Gross Domestic Product: the total value of goods and services produced in a country.

Inflation: a general rise in the level of prices over time.

24.02 Main stages of the business cycle

Economic growth is measured by changes in GDP.

Changes affect every business in an economy.

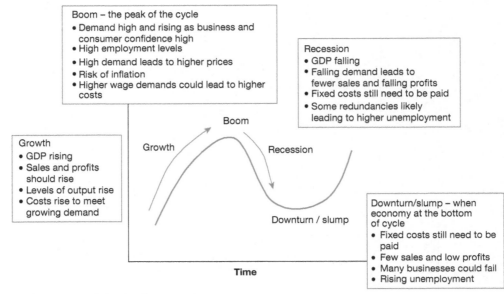

Boom – the peak of the cycle
- Demand high and rising as business and consumer confidence high
- High employment levels
- High demand leads to higher prices
- Risk of inflation
- Higher wage demands could lead to higher costs

Recession
- GDP falling
- Falling demand leads to fewer sales and falling profits
- Fixed costs still need to be paid
- Some redundancies likely leading to higher unemployment

Growth
- GDP rising
- Sales and profits should rise
- Levels of output rise
- Costs rise to meet growing demand

Downturn/slump – when economy at the bottom of cycle
- Fixed costs still need to be paid
- Few sales and low profits
- Many businesses could fail
- Rising unemployment

Growth · Boom · Recession · Downturn / slump · Time

Figure 24.01 The main stages of the business cycle.

TERMS

Business cycle: this refers to changes in the level of economic growth over time.

Economic boom: a period in the business cycle when economic growth is rising rapidly.

Economic growth: a period in the business cycle when GDP is rising.

Recession: a reduction in GDP over a period of time.

Slump: a prolonged period when GDP falls in an economy.

Sample question

HGB makes bicycles. The Finance Director has been looking at some financial information. She thinks that 2016 was a successful year as country X has had an economic recession and yet sales were good. HBG plans to invest in new machinery next year.

Define 'economic recession'. **[2]**

Sample answer:
An economic recession is a period in the business cycle when economic growth is falling. **[2]**

24.03 Impact of changes in taxation and government spending

Governments can encourage economic growth by:

- cutting taxes for individuals and businesses to encourage them to spend
- increasing the amount of government spending, for example on roads, hospitals.

Both actions should lead to MORE spending in the economy. Higher output will lead to an increase in GDP.

To slow down the rate of economic growth, a government could **increase** taxes or **reduce** government spending.

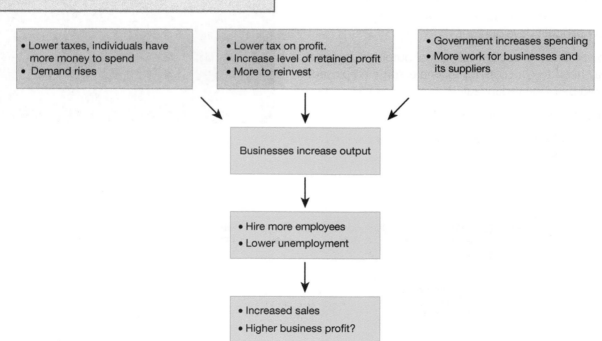

Figure 24.02 How changes in taxation and government spending can affect business activity.

24.04 Impact of changes in interest rates

An interest rate is the cost of borrowing money. Changing interest rates affects the amount of money that is available for people and businesses to spend or borrow.

A reduction in interest rates means the cost of borrowing is lower, so it is easier to access cheaper finance. Businesses benefit from lower expenses, and can afford to expand. The return on savings is also lower. More spending can increase business revenue.

An increase in interest rates has the opposite effect.

> **TIP**
> Lower interest rates have a similar effect to lower taxation and higher government spending.

24.05 How businesses might respond to changes in taxation and interest rates

What a business does will depend on its circumstances. Is the product or service a necessity or luxury? Is it a competitive market? Does the business need finance to expand?

- If demand falls, lower prices might encourage sales. Higher demand could see increased competition and new product development.

- Lower demand could mean lower output. A business may need to cut costs, for example, some employees could be made redundant.

- Interest rates will influence expansion plans.

- Demand for luxury products increases as disposable incomes rise.

Government aim:	Increase economic growth	Slow down rate of growth
Government action:	↓ taxation ↑ govt. spending ↓ interest rates	↑ taxation ↓ govt. spending ↑ interest rates
Effect on the economy:	↑ GDP ↓ unemployment ↑ inflation	↓ GDP ↑ unemployment ↓ inflation
Effect on businesses:	↑ sales ↑ profit Invest/hire more employees	↓ sales ↓ profit Reduce size/close down

Table 24.01 The effect of government influence.

Progress check

1 Define 'inflation'.

2 Identify **three** government economic objectives.

3 Identify the **four** stages of the business cycle.

4 What is likely to happen to finance costs if interest rates rise?

Summary

Changes in the business cycle affect businesses. Governments will try to achieve their economic objectives through changes to tax, spending and interest rate policies. These changes will impact businesses in terms of costs, sales and profits.

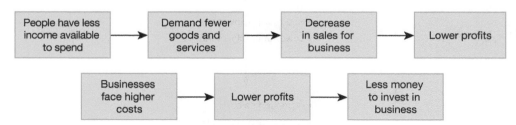

Figure 24.03 The effect of an increase in interest rates.

Sample questions

NPC builds low-cost housing. The business has had a successful year in 2015, and achieved its main objective as profits increased by $12m. The Operations Director cannot decide how the latest economic data will affect NPC.

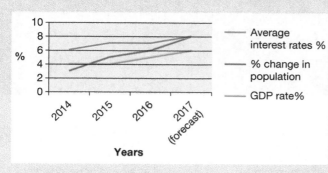

Figure 24.04 Extract of economic data for 2014–2017.

Example 1:
Identify **two** economic objectives (other than economic growth) that a government might have. **[2]**

Sample answer:
Objective 1: Lower unemployment. [1]
Objective 2: Positive balance of payments. [1]

Example 2:
Explain **two** possible ways the economic data might affect NPC. **[8]**

Sample answer:
Way 1: The population is rising [1] from 3% to 8% [1]. As people will need somewhere to live [1], there should be increased demand for building materials and sales [1].

Way 2: Interest rates have risen [1] over the past three years to 8% [1]. This will increase the cost of borrowing [1] so if people are worried, they may look to buy low-cost housing as this is a less expensive option [1].

Examination-style questions

Country G is enjoying an economic boom. Employment is high and many new businesses are starting up. DLZ makes a range of electrical products including washing machines and ovens. Due to increased demand, DLZ plans to recruit another 200 skilled employees. The Managing Director said, 'This is a good time for business. Profits are high. Why can't the government find another way to influence business activity, rather than always increasing taxation?'

a Define 'economic boom'. [2]

b Identify **two** ways (other than taxation) that a government could influence business activity.
Way 1:
Way 2: [2]

c Explain **two** ways in which higher taxation might affect DLZ.
Way 1:
Way 2: [6]

d Explain **two** ways (other than taxation) in which an economic boom might affect DLZ.
Way 1:
Way 2: [8]

Environmental and ethical issues

Learning summary

By the end of this unit you should understand:

- ☐ how business activity can impact on the environment, and the concept of externalities

- ☐ the concept of sustainable development

- ☐ how and why a business might respond to environmental pressures and opportunities

- ☐ ethical issues a business might face, and how a business might react and respond.

25.01 How business activity can impact on the environment

Business activity produces goods and services to satisfy people's needs and wants. This can damage the environment.

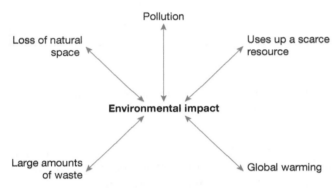

Figure 25.01 How business activity can impact on the environment.

Externalities

When making important decisions, a business often focuses on the costs and benefits to the business; for example, the cost of the machinery, value of additional sales.

Externalities refer to the impact of business activity on others outside the business. The impact can be positive (**external benefit**) or negative (**external cost**). Table 25.01 has examples.

External benefits	External costs
Jobs created in the community	Environmental factors such as air and noise pollution
Improved facilities such as schools and hospitals	Destruction of natural habitats for wildlife and locals to use
New or improved roads are built	Increased risk of global warming from cutting down trees/burning coal
Regeneration of areas if new businesses are attracted	Social factors such as loss of local jobs if another business has to close

Table 25.01 Example of costs and benefits from externalities.

Some businesses set objectives to reduce the impact of environmental damage. Managers will consider the impact of externalities when making decisions.

 TIP Externalities can be positive or negative. Unless a question states benefits or costs, you can discuss either.

 TIP Global warming is the increase in average world temperatures caused by pollution.

Sample question

Blue Tigers is a football club. Each week, 60 000 people visit from across the country to watch sports matches or music events in the stadium. The Chief Executive said, 'This is a community club so it is important that we try to limit external costs if we can.'

Explain **two** external costs Blue Tigers might create. **[6]**

Sample answer:

External cost 1: Litter: as 60 000 people visit each week, this can damage the image of the area, deterring people to visit at other times. **[3]**

External cost 2: Noise pollution, as football matches and music events will be loud. This can disturb local residents, especially if the event happens at night. **[3]**

25.02 Sustainable development

> ### TERM
>
> Sustainable development: trying to meet the needs of the present population without damaging the ability of future generations to meet their own needs.

Sustainable development involves trying to balance meeting consumer demands without ignoring environmental, social and economic issues. Businesses can contribute by:

- reducing resources used, for example, lean production, limiting amount of packaging

- recycling materials such as water or unused parts

- developing new techniques and materials for production

- using renewable sources of energy, for example, wind, solar or hydro-power

- reducing the amount of travel – use technology and source materials locally.

25.03 Environmental pressures and opportunities

Businesses have to respond to environmental issues. This will cost money but can also offer opportunities.

Opportunities	Pressures
• Competitive advantage • Better image and reputation can increase sales	• Takes time to adapt processes to be environmentally friendly
• New markets, as customers demand 'environmentally friendly' products	• Might not be able to source materials any other way
• New production techniques • Can also cut wastage and lower costs	• Increased business costs can reduce profit
• Meet legal controls / avoid fines if pollution is reduced	• Higher prices to cover costs can reduce sales

Table 25.02 Environmental pressures and opportunities on businesses.

Role of pressure groups

By raising awareness about an issue, pressure groups hope that it can influence the business. Businesses can ignore pressure groups, but risk damaging their reputation and sales.

> ### TIP
>
> Pressure groups have no powers to make laws. They can only influence others.

> ### TERM
>
> Pressure group: a group of people who come together with a common aim to try to influence the activities and decisions of businesses or government.

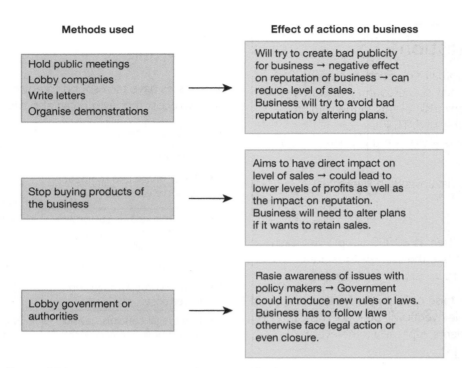

Methods used	Effect of actions on business
Hold public meetings Lobby companies Write letters Organise demonstrations	Will try to create bad publicity for business → negative effect on reputation of business → can reduce level of sales. Business will try to avoid bad reputation by altering plans.
Stop buying products of the business	Aims to have direct impact on level of sales → could lead to lower levels of profits as well as the impact on reputation. Business will need to alter plans if it wants to retain sales.
Lobby govenrment or authorities	Rasie awareness of issues with policy makers → Government could introduce new rules or laws. Business has to follow laws otherwise face legal action or even closure.

Figure 25.02 The effects which pressure groups can have on a business.

Role of legal controls

Governments can influence business activity through a range of measures:

- **Pollution permits** – these give businesses a legal right to pollute a certain amount. If a business can reduce its pollution, the permit can be sold to other businesses.

- **Legal controls** – these set standards for production and waste disposal.

- **Planning restrictions** – so that the business can only operate in certain locations.

- **Taxation**.

25.04 Ethical issues a business might face and how it may respond

> **TIP**
> Ethical is not the same as legal. Laws cannot be ignored. A business can choose to be ethical or not.

An ethical business will consider the impact of its decisions on all its stakeholders, not just shareholders.

Decisions to be made	The impact of those decisions
What level of wages to pay employee?	Paying the minimum wage might not be a living wage
Should child labour be used?	Using children can be seen as exploitation
Should operations move to a country with lower legal standards? Should the business worry whether suppliers act in an ethical way?	Standards vary between countries. A business could lower its operating costs while remaining legal Business may pay fair wages, but do its suppliers have similarly high ethical standards?
What is a fair price to pay suppliers? What materials should be used to make products – are they responsibly sourced?	Higher variable costs could lead to higher prices, so the business is not as competitive

Table 25.03 The impact of decisions on stakeholders.

> **TERM**
> Ethics: behaving in a way which is right and fair.

Ethics and profit can clash. Ethical behaviour can increase business costs, which can lower profit.

However, being ethical does not automatically mean lower profits.

- The business could be seen as a good employer by improving work conditions and paying fair wages. It could then be easier to retain and recruit employees.

- More 'fair trade' schemes are available (which guarantee a fair price to suppliers).

- Pressure groups campaign against businesses which exploit child labour and employees. This damages their brand image, and sales could fall.

- An ethical brand image can increase the business's reputation. Customers can be willing to pay more for ethical goods, therefore sales increase.

Progress check

1. Identify **two** ways in which a business can affect the environment.

2. Identify the **two** types of externalities.

3. What is sustainable development?

4. What is the difference between 'legal' and 'ethical'?

Summary

Business activity creates externalities, including its impact on the environment. Pressure groups and legal controls can influence business behaviour. A business will also have to react and respond to a number of ethical issues.

Sample questions

HBC makes mobile phones. Sales continue to increase, despite HBC operating in a very competitive market. HBC imports most of its components from low-cost countries. HBC tries to adopt an ethical approach to business issues. The Managing Director said, 'Globalisation is good for business. It would be better if there were no import quotas.'

Example 1:
Explain **two** ethical issues HBC might face. [6]

Sample answer:
Issue 1: What is a fair price to pay suppliers [1]? It is a competitive market [1], so HBC will want to keep its prices low to remain competitive [1].

Issue 2: Should HBC be concerned about how suppliers treat its employees [1] who are based in low-cost countries [1]? Are the conditions and pay fair [1]?

Example 2:
Explain **two** possible advantages to HBC of being ethical. [8]

Sample answer:
Benefit 1: The business will have a better reputation [1] so customers may pay more for its phones [1]. This will help HBC to remain competitive [1], so sales can continue to rise [1].

Benefit 2: Suppliers are happy to provide inventory [1] as they receive a fair price [1]. The business will be less likely to run out of components [1], which is important when most of the inventory is imported [1].

Examination-style questions

TUP is a private limited company. One of its objectives is profit. TUP makes low-cost building blocks from recycling waste plastic. TUP rents an old factory near the city centre. Materials are delivered most days. Demand has increased quickly from 1000 to 25 000 blocks per week. The Production manager is worried about pressure groups. 'TUP creates many externalities. I need deliveries every day now as well as 30 more employees. TUP may need a new site!' He believes that most stakeholders will benefit from the increase in production.

a   Define 'pressure group'.   [2]

b   Explain **two** externalities TUP might create.
    Externality 1:
    Externality 2:   [6]

c   Explain **two** ways that a pressure group might try to influence TUP's decisions.
    Way 1:
    Way 2:   [8]

Business and the international economy

26.01 Globalisation

The world is now one large market. Countries have become dependent on each other, leading to the expansion of trade.

Reasons for globalisation include:

- improvements in technology, transport and communications

- limited resources in some countries, so some items have to be imported

- rising living standards so people can afford and want more product choice

- the removal of trade barriers.

Opportunities	Threats
Access to larger markets can increase sales and spread risk.	Increased competition could reduce sales for domestic businesses.
Access to a greater variety of resources and products means that the business can supply more choices.	Marketing and distribution costs increase in a worldwide market.
Businesses may set up operations in other countries, benefiting from higher skills and/or lower costs.	There is a risk of closure and job losses for local businesses.

Table 26.01 Opportunities and threats posed by globalisation.

TERM

Globalisation: integration of economies due to trade, investment and movement of people and resources.

26.02 Why governments introduce import tariffs and quotas

Most governments want to encourage trade. More choice and lower prices are good for consumers. Tax revenue and new jobs can help to achieve the government's economic objectives.

Tariffs and quotas are sometimes used to protect domestic businesses from overseas competition.

- **Tariffs** are a form of tax. Imported goods become less competitive as they are more expensive to buy. They are also a source of government revenue.

- **Quotas** restrict the number of goods that can be imported. These are often used to protect industries starting up, so they have time to become established.

TERMS

Quotas: a physical limit on the amount of goods allowed in a country.

Tariffs: import taxes put on the price of goods entering the country.

26.03 Reasons for the importance and growth of multinational companies

Globalisation means that there are often a small number of very large businesses competing against each other. A multinational company (MNC) has its headquarters in one country and operations in many other (host) countries around the world. Decisions taken by a MNC affect a large number of people and countries.

26.04 Benefits to a business of becoming a multinational company

- **Access to a global market** – can increase sales and market share.

- **Spread risk** – less reliant on a market that may be limited in size or in decline.

- **Lower transport and distribution costs** – as produce is near the target market.

- **Access to cheaper sources of materials and labour.**

- **Economies of scale.**

- **Avoid legal and trade barriers.**

- **Remain competitive in a global market.**

Benefits are similar to any large business. It is where a MNC operates that is different.

26.05 Potential benefits and drawbacks to a host country and/or its economy where an MNC operates

Benefits	Drawbacks
Jobs created will lower unemployment and improve living standards.	Jobs are often unskilled and low paid.
The country will be less reliant on imports as there will be access to a wider range of products made locally.	There could be reduced sales for local businesses that cannot compete, leading to job losses and closure.
Access to new technology and expertise.	The MNC might use up scarce resources.
Taxes can be used for government services.	Profits are sent back to the MNC's home country.
Increased choice and lower prices (no duties or additional transport costs).	Loss of cultural identity, as standard products are sold everywhere.

Benefits	Drawbacks
Infrastructure improvements to roads.	MNC can influence government decisions.
Improved image for the country could lead to additional investment.	The MNC has no loyalty to the country, so could easily leave if it saw better opportunities elsewhere.

Table 26.02 Benefits and drawbacks for a country hosting an MNC.

TERM

Multinational company (MNC): a business with factories, production or service operations in more than one country.

26.06 Impact on stakeholders of becoming an MNC

Benefits	Drawbacks
Growth increases profits and could increase wages.	Managers might have to relocate to host country.
Growth provides greater job security for employees.	Some production might be moved to host country which threatens job security.
More opportunities for promotion.	Greater risk of failure which could reduce profits and hence dividends and share price for shareholders.
Increase dividend/share price for shareholders.	Larger company could be more difficult to manage. Could increase managers' workload.
If financed by borrowing then lenders have increased revenue/profits.	

Table 26.03 Benefits and drawbacks for stakeholders of a company becoming an MNC.

26.07 The impact of exchange rates

Exchange rates influence the price of imports and exports. A change in the value of one currency will affect a business in terms of sales, costs and profit.

The appreciation of a currency (rise in value) means it is worth **more**, relative to another currency. Importers can buy more with same amount of money. This can be a problem for exporters, as its customers have to pay more to buy their products.

A depreciation of a currency (fall in value) means it is worth **less**, relative to another currency. Goods are relatively cheaper, so exports are more competitive. Importers have to pay more.

	Currency appreciation	Currency depreciation
Importer	Imports cheaper. ↓ prices could fall ↑ sales ↑ profits	Imports more expensive. ↑ prices may rise ↓ sales ↓ profits
Exporter	Exports more expensive. ↑ prices may rise ↓ sales ↓ profits	Exports cheaper. ↓ prices could fall ↑ sales ↑ profits

Table 26.04 Advantages and disadvantages of currency appreciation and depreciation for importers and exporters.

Worked example

Imagine an exchange rate of 1$ = 10R.

1   A toy that costs 10$ will sell for 100R.

2   A business importing parts costing 100R would pay 10$.

If the value of 1$ fell to 5R, how would this affect the two businesses?

1   The toy would cost 50R so exports would be cheaper.

2   The parts would now cost 20$. Imports will cost more.

Sample question

Denzel owns a successful sweet factory based in Europe. He imports high quality sugar from Mauritius to make his products.

Outline how an appreciation in the exchange rate might affect Denzel's business. **[4]**

Sample answer:
This will reduce import prices, making it cheaper for Denzel to buy sugar so he could lower costs. This would allow him to increase his profit margin, because he might not want to lower the price as it could damage the luxury image. **[4]**

Progress check

1   What is the difference between a tariff and a quota?

2   Identify **two** reasons for a business to become a multinational company.

3   Is any business that sells goods overseas called a multinational? Explain.

4   Does currency depreciation help or hinder exporters?

Summary

Globalisation offers both opportunities and threats to businesses. Governments can use quotas and tariffs to protect local businesses. The growth of multinational companies brings both advantages and disadvantages. The impact of exchange rates will affect all businesses involved in international trade.

Sample questions

HBC makes mobile phones. Sales continue to increase, despite HBC operating in a very competitive market. HBC imports most of its components from low-cost countries. HBC tries to adopt an ethical approach to business issues. The Managing Director said, 'Globalisation is good for business. It would be better if there were no import quotas.'

Example 1:
Outline how import quotas might affect HBC. **[4]**

Sample answer:
This will limit the amount of components HBC can bring into the country **[1]**. Fewer components would mean fewer phones could be made **[1]**. This would reduce output, making it harder for HBC to compete **[1]**, so sales might start to fall **[1]**.

Example 2:
Explain **two** advantages to HBC of importing inventory. **[8]**

Sample answer:
Advantage 1: Better quality **[1]**. This might help HBC to be more competitive **[1]** as customers will see that the components make the product last longer **[1]**. This could allow HBC to charge higher prices if necessary **[1]**.

Advantage 2: Lower costs **[1]**. As it buys from low-cost countries **[1]**, HBC could sell its phones at lower prices **[1]** and increase sales and profit **[1]**.

Example 3:
Explain **two** possible problems (other than import quotas) for HBC of importing inventory. **[6]**

Sample answer:
Problem 1: Tariffs, as they will increase the price of components. This can increase the cost of sales. **[3]**

Problem 2: Delays due to distance could cause inventory to arrive late. This may mean that the production of phones has to stop. **[3]**

Examination-style questions

SGK is a multinational company. It makes a range of healthcare products including toothpaste and shampoo. It plans to open a new factory in country C. Unemployment is high, but market research shows there could be a large target market here. SGK expects there to be a lot of competition. The new factory will employ 400 workers. The Managing Director said, 'Everyone can benefit. SGK will not have to worry so much about import tariffs and exchange rates.'

a Define 'import tariff'. [2]

b Explain **two** possible advantages to SGK of operating in country C.

Advantage 1:
Advantage 2: [6]

c Explain how each of the following could affect SGK if they do not set up operations in country C.
Appreciation of country C's currency:
Import tariffs: [8]

d Explain how each of the following **three** factors might affect country C if SGK set up there. Which factor do you think will affect country C the most? Justify your answer.
Jobs:
Pollution:
Competition:
Conclusion: [12]

Answers to progress check and examination-style questions

All answers that appear in this publication have been written by the author.

Unit 1

Progress check

1 Limited availability of resources to meet the unlimited wants of people.

2 We must satisfy needs to live, such as food. Things which we like but are not essential are wants, such as a certain style of shoes.

3 The purpose of business activity is to provide the goods and services that people need or want.

4 Space for stall; person to run stall; till or table to display goods.

Examination-style questions

a Opportunity cost is the cost of something in terms of the next best option not selected.

b Land, labour, capital or enterprise.

c It can charge more; differentiate itself from its rivals; lower costs as it will have a better reputation.

d Branding; reduce costs with same price; add extra features; improved service.

Application for c and d might include: cars or related terms, such as satnav, tyres, delivery; luxury, competitive market.

Unit 2

Progress check

1 Public sector.

2 Manufacturing, building, refining.

3 Primary: mining; Secondary: jeweller who makes ring; Tertiary: retailer.

4 A public sector business is owned by government. Private sector business is owned and controlled by individuals.

Examination-style questions

1 a Primary: farming, forestry, mining; Secondary: food processing, refining.

b 21 million.

c Country B has limited natural resources – primary sector only 10% (45% in A) – so fewer

jobs are available; nearly three-quarters of jobs are in the service sector; 70% (35% in A) – these might have specialist skills; cheaper food sources in B so less need for primary sector; the primary sector is mechanised so there are fewer jobs; large public sector – health and education sectors.

Application involves use of numbers.

2 SRT options include: **Banking** – need an account to make and receive payments more easily. **Advertising agency** – to help promote products and increase customers' awareness / remind customers. **Insurance** – need to protect against accidents: if the business is not liable, legal action could damage reputation. **Accountants** – manage its accounts. **Legal services** – if any customers complain about their products. **Transport businesses** – to get products to and from the retail outlets.

Application for 2 could include: paint or associated terms such as colour, tins; many countries; market research.

Unit 3

Progress check

1 Someone who organises, operates and takes the risk for a new business venture.

2 A capital-intensive business uses a lot of machines, so few employees are needed.

3 Sell more of current product in existing markets; sell current product in new markets/segments; launch a new product; adapt an existing product.

4 Personal reasons, lack of finance, size of market.

Examination-style questions

a Two of: value of sales, value of output, capital employed, employees.

b Helps planning, applying for loans, help decision-making.

c The business will be harder to manage and control; communication problems could arise, so orders lost; motivation – lower productivity or employees leave;

financial or cash flow problems; effect on ownership – they might have to give up some control.

d   Points could include: **Join with another business** – quicker way to grow - able to benefit from advantages of growth (economies of scale, spread risk) quicker, harder to control as businesses have different objectives, could lose control of business. **Expand its product range** – able to control, relatively inexpensive as able to use own resources, very slow process - so could lose out on business opportunities. Recommendation based on points discussed.

Application for questions b–d could include: glass or related terms, for example bottles, screens, windows; successful, partnership, business plan, develop new products, old factory.

Unit 4

Progress check

1   Sole trader has one owner, a partnership has at least two partners.

2   The owner is responsible for the business debts, so their personal assets are at risk if they cannot pay business debts.

3   A franchise is an agreement that allows one business to trade under the name of another business, to sell the other company's products or services.

4   Joint ventures remain as separate companies. Mergers join to become a larger business.

Examination-style questions

a   A business whose shares cannot be sold to the general public.

b   The business will only lose the amount invested in the business, not personal assets.

c   No need to publish (detailed) accounts; limited liability; control over who can buy shares; easier to raise money; more credibility with suppliers; separate legal identity; continuity after death of owners.

d   Points could include: **Private limited** – limited liability, continuity of existence, able to sell shares, easier to keep control than PLC as can control who sell shares to, have to disclose limited financial information (compared to PLC); need agreement of other shareholders to sell shares, restricted number of shareholders, cannot sell shares on stock exchange - limits amount can raise compared to PLC.

Public limited – additional access to funds; can sell shares to public – status; more legal formalities to complete – time and cost; have to disclose full accounts – rivals gain information about business; risk of takeover. Recommendation based on points discussed.

Application for questions c–d includes: expand into Asia, farm equipment such as tractors and trailers, private limited company, competitive market, $10m.

Unit 5

Progress check

1   Objectives provide a target for the business to work towards.

2   The business priority of a social enterprise is achieving social objectives. Any profit made is reinvested back into business or community projects.

3   Profit, survival, break-even.

4   Provide a service, control natural monopolies and protect key industries.

Examination-style questions

a   Any group of individuals who have an interest in the activities of a business.

b   Profit, growth, increased sales or market share.

c   Profits – ARG wants profit so they sell to customers willing to pay their prices. Cut jobs to increase profit. Government – aim is service which is cheap, accessible to all. Want jobs to ensure lower unemployment.

d   Options include: owner/shareholders are sources of finance; employees or managers carry out/control day-to-day operations; customers buy what the business makes; banks/lenders provide an important source of finance; government can restrict how the business operates.

Application for questions c–d includes: food retailer, takeover, use of numbers, competitive market, demands changing, technology.

Unit 6

Progress check

1   Motivated employees are likely to produce more, produce better quality work and are less likely to leave.

2   Pay, safe conditions and reasonable hours.

3 Physical, safety, social, self esteem and self fulfilment.

4 Commission is based on how many sold. Piece rate is based on the number made.

Examination-style questions

a Options include: job rotation, job enrichment, job enlargement, team work, promotion.

b Either viewpoint possible if supported. Issues include: praise is an example of self esteem; employees might enjoy knowing they are part of the reason for business success; recognition only works if other needs already met. If they want or need more money, praise will not motivate them. What motivates each individual differs - some might want more responsibility rather than praise. Evaluation: It is unlikely that praise can work on its own.

c Advantage: pay only for hours worked - reduce labour costs; employees will take time to look after customers – not in a rush so this helps improve the business's reputation. Disadvantage: slow employees – so takes longer to complete tasks, damaging service level.

d Points could include: **Bonuses** – work harder to meet targets to earn extra money. Not guaranteed. Impact of external factors (for example, recession, bad weather). **Job enrichment** – work more challenging / employees feel valued so self esteem increases; training costs. Able to add variety. **Fringe benefits** – extra incentives. Can boost morale, and pride in work; insurance meets security need; employees might expect benefits though, so how effective is it? Would cost money so business could increase prices. Conclusion based on points discussed.

Application for questions b–d could include: praise, holidays for families, weather, seasonal business, activities, democratic leadership style, important to success, awards for customer service and health and safety, competitive prices.

Unit 7

Progress check

1 An organisation chart shows lines of communication, everyone's role, relationships between departments and people.

2 Size, skills of employee and manager, type of work.

3 By product, function, region.

4 Quicker to respond, better motivation.

Examination-style questions

a A group of employees who join together to protect the interests of its members.

b Can react more quickly to changes in demand; more competitive; suit customer tastes in local area; increase sales or reputation; improve employee motivation; higher output or performance.

c Advantages: time for managers to focus on other tasks; help motivate others as work is more interesting; help retain employees as there is more variety in the work; train future managers; use individual expertise so improve service; speed up decision-making. Disadvantages: time wasted explaining task so benefits are limited; managers feel threatened so working relationships damaged; managers not fully aware so could make wrong decisions on other matters; mistakes of inexperienced subordinates can be expensive to correct.

d Points could include: **Autocratic** – quicker decision-making so react quicker to demand; clear direction so less duplication and less wasted resources; employees lack motivation so lower quality/mistakes made; employees cannot develop skills; slow work while await decision so lower output. **Democratic** – employees more involved so motivation improves; takes time so can slow production; can encourage loyalty; able to spot potential so could use internal recruitment in future which is cheaper. **Laissez-faire** – high motivation; employees use skills but no real direction so problems of coordination; conflict between team members could lower output; depends on skills of manager; work and type of work done. Conclusion based on points discussed.

Application for questions b–d could include: furniture, skilled work (hand-finished), region, delegation, trade unions, autocratic, sells nationally.

Unit 8

Progress check

1 Job description, person specification, advertising, interviewing and selection.

2 Induction training introduces new employees to the business and its procedures.

3 Off-the-job happens away from workplace, by experts. On-the-job takes place at a workstation, by another employee.

4 Legal controls ensure the fair treatment of employees.

Examination-style questions

a Employees learn job-specific skills while they are working.

b Minimum wages, health and safety (or examples of), employment contract, protection against discrimination.

c More flexible so able to cover when someone not available; helps to meet demand during busy times so able to offer good service; helps to extend opening hours so able to remain popular; can fit around employees' other commitments so might help attract new employees; only paid when needed so lower labour costs; can add more skills/ experience to the business.

d **Job description** – outlines the tasks and responsibilities of a specific job, so applicants know what the job involves – saves time as unsuitable applications avoided. **Person specification** – outlines the required qualifications, personal qualities for specific job, so suitably qualified person is appointed with right skills for job required. **Advertisement** – informs people of job vacancy – what job involves, qualifications, and so on, so only suitable candidates apply; placed where suitable applicants might see it.

Application for questions b–d could include: 45 rooms, six other hotels, 20 full-time, 40 part-time, on-the-job training, fitness centre, increase revenue, long hours, seasonal demand.

Unit 9

Progress check

1 Pass and receive messages, give instruction, check feedback and discuss.

2 Check understanding, instant response, use of body language.

3 What the message is, why it is being sent, who it is sent to, speed and need for written evidence.

4 One-way gives no opportunity for feedback, unlike two-way communication.

Examination-style questions

a Any factor which causes a breakdown in communication.

b Better coordination, fewer mistakes, motivate employees, avoid duplication, ensure that inventory is available on time.

c Answer depends on options selected – include letter, email, meeting, text.

d Points could include: **Meeting** – two-way, chance for feedback, able to discuss ideas, can involve a large number of people; no guarantee that everyone is listening or had chance to ask questions. **Email** – quick and easy to use, copy for reference; can send to many people at same time; no guarantee that content is understood if language not suitable; people might not receive it. **Telephone** – feedback, chance to discuss issues; expensive in time and cost of calls especially if contacting many people; danger of giving different message to different people, so adding to confusion. Recommendation based on points discussed.

Application for questions b–d could include: carpets, large shops, four suppliers, barriers to communication, inventory control, reduce costs.

Unit 10

Progress check

1 Identify, anticipate and satisfy demand; make a profit.

2 Small market, limited growth, specialised products.

3 Segregation can help with promotion, spotting gaps and developing products to better match customer needs.

4 Loss of traditional products, cut costs by lower quality.

Examination-style questions

a It is the specific group or segment of customers that the product is directed at.

b Benefits include: help to build business's reputation, increase sales, cheaper than trying to attract new customers, source of information.

c Points include: identify customer needs – know what they want from the business; satisfy customer needs – to encourage them to return; anticipate changes in customer needs so he is able to provide for them and adapt what he offers; raise awareness so people know; advertise to persuade customers or attract attention.

d Points could include: **Loyalty schemes** – so customers have an incentive to return, but there are costs and a risk to image. **Ask for feedback** – knows how to improve – this takes time; **Train employees** – reduce mistakes - able to provide better service, cost of training, time to train. Recommendation based on points discussed.

Application for questions b–d could include: new, teacher, qualified, 14–16-year-olds, primary research, tutoring, some demand, exams.

Unit 11

Progress check

1 It is a small number of people who represent the target market, who meet regularly to give their views on products or issues.

2 Bias can produce misleading results, so wrong decisions are made.

3 It is not feasible in terms of time and cost to ask all customers for their views.

4 Visual representation – easy to see relative importance of each segment; easy to understand.

Examination-style questions

a Little use if it is inaccurate/irrelevant/inappropriate – wrong people asked or wrong information gathered; bias in research (how questions are asked); / sample size too small; tastes change over time.

b See Figure 27.01. For all marks the student must include title and label axes.

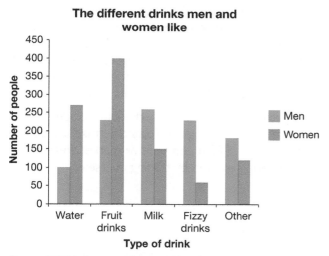

The different drinks men and women like

Figure 27.01 Answer to question b.

c Points include: make decisions about what to produce – so avoid waste; decide on prices to charge – more likely to sell; know potential size of market – so whether it is worth developing a new product; find out where to sell – convenient for consumers to buy.

d Points could include: **Government sources** – cheap to collect, accurate as official data, cover wide range of information but may be out of date or not provide information needed. **Internet research of competitors' websites** – cheap to collect, quick to collect, may be out of date, not all competitors have website, not include all want to know.

Market research reports – fee payable, detailed information. Recommendation based on points discussed.

For questions c–d application could include: types of drinks, use of data, older people, reduce the cost, 2000 people.

Unit 12

Progress check

1 Student's own answer based on choices made.

2 Introduction, growth, maturity and decline.

3 It guarantees a certain amount of profit; when not in a competitive market.

4 Sales would rise by less than percentage change in price, so lower profits likely.

Examination-style question

a The stages a product will pass through from its introduction to growth to the end of the product's time in the market.

b Packaging would protect from damage, inform customers how to use it, promote the product and raise awareness, boost brand image as easily recognised, be easy to store.

c Advantages include: spread risk as not relying on one product for sales; increase sales as more choice; attract new customers so increase customer base; technology allows new products so remain competitive. Disadvantages include: will damage image if the product is not liked; costs of development, marketing, production; increases risk of failure.

d A positive brand image can encourage loyalty so more customers are willing to try other products it makes; differentiates product from rivals; the business can charge a higher price so is able to recover development costs quicker; increases sales as customers are attracted to the name.

e Points could include: **Target different market segment** – customer base widens. **Add new features** – more attractive to existing/new customers. **Change packaging** – it seems like a new product. Recommendation based on points discussed.

For questions b–e, application could include: electrical products, cameras, phones, red packaging, brand image, decline stage, best-selling, competitive market.

Unit 13

Progress check

1 Producer – consumer.

2 An agent is used when selling overseas.

3 Cost, type of product, stage in product life cycle, target market (how, where and how many), competitor's actions, strategy.

4 E-commerce, promotion, type of products.

Examination-style questions

a Money which the business plans to use for marketing purposes for a certain time period.

b E-commerce, promotion, type of products.

c Television – attracts a large audience; specialist magazines to target specific customers; social media – can attract instant attention; billboards/posters catch the eye of people passing; leaflets – can keep them for later reference.

d Student's own answer based on points made. Advantages include: E-commerce: customers can make bookings when convenient to them; attracts wider target market – possible to advertise around the world; lower printing costs as customers access information online; lower labour costs as fewer people are needed to deal with customer requests; market research to compare prices/services with competitors; most people use technology today; gain feedback from customers so the business knows how to improve. Disadvantages include: not everyone has internet access so sales could be lost; lot of competition so customers could miss website; loss of personal contact might damage quality; need experts to manage website.

For questions b–d, application could include: 40 hotels, 70% business people, good reputation, offers competitive prices, $3m, ten more hotels, website.

Unit 14

Progress check

1 Product, price, promotion and place.

2 Increase sales, increase revenue, increase market share, enter new market.

3 None – it is important to have the right balance between all four.

4 Spread risk, increased market, increased recognition.

Examination-style questions

a A marketing strategy is a plan of actions a business will take to achieve its marketing objectives.

b Spread risk, increase customer base, increase market share/sales, fewer trade restrictions, greater recognition.

c Points could include: **Product:** must be long-lasting and durable as breakages could damage their reputation and sales. After-sales support so that repairs could be done quickly. **Price:** this depends on the quality and cost of equipment. Cost plus pricing as it would ensure that some profit is made. Competitive pricing if there are many rivals, to ensure sufficient sales. Penetration pricing – new market so would help establish sales. **Promotion:** specialist magazines to attract suitable customers; trade fairs as large number of buyers. Sales promotions might encourage sales. **Place:** directly to customers, retailers can widen their potential market; trade fairs as they target specific customer base.

d Points could include: **Agent** – knowledge but commission payable. Does not avoid exchange rate or trade barriers. **Joint venture** – pool resources, share expertise but profits are shared and decisions could lead to conflict. **Licensing** – saves costs of factory and transport but there are control and quality issues. Recommendation based on points discussed.

Application for questions b–d could include reference to farming and related terms for example, soil, farmers, $20m, competitive market, small engineering, expand by trading overseas.

Unit 15

Progress check

1 The business uses a high proportion of labour (employees) to produce goods.

2 To eliminate waste throughout the production process.

3 Flow, as employees have to do simple monotonous tasks.

4 CAM, CAD, automation.

Examination-style questions

a The business uses a high proportion of machinery to make goods.

b Options include: training so employees know how to do the job better; automation, as machines can work continuously; update machinery as it will be less likely to break down; improve motivation so employees are willing to produce more / make fewer mistakes.

c Options include: less wastage so the business can reduce the level of inventory needed; it motivates employees as they are involved in the process; lower costs of rent as space is saved; less risk of obsolescence as only necessary materials are purchased.

d Points could include: **Just in time** – no need to store inventory, saving space and cost; depends on suppliers being able to deliver when needed. **Cell production** – can help motivate employees, can see who is responsible for production. **Kaizen** – more likely to know how to improve production, small changes only. Recommendation based on points discussed.

Application for questions b–d could include: lorries or related terms or parts, buy locally, tyres imported, 250 factory workers efficient to be competitive, high rent and storage costs, many employees leave, capital-intensive, same job.

Unit 16

Progress check

1 Fixed costs do not change with output but variable costs do.

2 Set prices, whether to stop or change level of production, location.

3 Communication problems, lack of effective control, motivation issues.

4 It is the difference between the current level of output and break-even output.

Examination-style questions

a Costs that do not vary with the level of output or sales.

b (i) 45 000 / (6 − 3) = 15 000

(ii) Revenue (30 000 × 6) − Total costs (30 000 × 3 + 45 000) = 45 000

c Student's own answer based on points discussed. Points include: positive contribution helps towards fixed costs; makes a profit; depends if demand rising or falling as this might affect revenue and prices charged; Product A makes greater profit.

d Technical as the business can afford specialist equipment; purchasing – receive discounts for buying in bulk; can afford to hire specialist managers so able to make better decisions; financial, as seen as lower risk to lenders.

Application for questions c–d could include: use of data, animal feed, horses, chickens.

Unit 17

Progress check

1 Student's own answer. Points might include: materials, brand, lasts long time, does what it says it will.

2 Quality control takes place at the end of production, assurance avoid errors throughout.

3 Points include: cost of rework and waste materials, poor reputation, time delays, lost orders.

4 Throughout the process.

Examination-style questions

a Checking products at the end of the production process to see if they meet the set standard.

b Points include: cost of rework and wasted ingredients, poor reputation, time delays, lost orders.

c Quality control – prevent poor quality products reaching customers; other methods such as quality assurance, training, improve motivation so employees stop making errors or spot them earlier; ask for feedback to see what customers want; see what competitors do; new equipment so the business is able to produce a better range / on time.

d Points could include: **Train employees** – less likely to make mistakes but could still be some errors, lower cost of rework, cost and time to train as all involved probably best option. **Quality control** – know no errors, only check at end so mistakes still expensive to correct, cost of person to check. **Better quality ingredients** – help establish quality image, good chance of good output, materials can still be wasted if process poor, higher cost of sales, mistakes more expensive to correct. Conclusion based on points discussed.

Application for questions b–d could include: food or related words such as biscuits, cakes, flavour, ingredients, 45 employees, machines break down, new technology.

Unit 18

Progress check

1   Points include: cost, customers, suppliers, competition, legislation, the environment, infrastructure, available workforce.

2   Options include: competition, access to parking, customers, cost of site, labour.

3   Certain products like foodstuff need specific conditions to grow.

4   Grants, where the business is allowed to locate, restrictions on how to operate.

Examination-style questions

a   Financial incentives, for example grants, rent rebates, tax incentives; legislation.

b   To maintain brand image, provide access to customers, be near competitors, keep costs low.

c   Student's own answer based on points raised. Issues could include points listed in b. Other factors: product – what customers want and quality of service; promotion – to attract attention; pricing – so customers can afford to pay.

d   Points could include: **Land** – cost and space as hotel will take up a large area - needs to be near where business people want to stay - so could be expensive - can they afford it. **Labour** – skilled/access to employees - as need to offer good service to maintain reputation as 40 other hotels, can be trained. **Competitors** – close could help attract/lose potential customers as choice, limited influence over actions of rivals. Conclusion based on points discussed.

Application for questions b–d could include: 40 hotels, ten new hotels, good reputation, competitive prices, increase sales, website, two years.

Unit 19

Progress check

1   Start-up capital, working capital, capital expenditure.

2   Finance which comes from within the business.

3   A loan is a debt that needs to be repaid with interest; shares represent ownership so no interest is due but the shareholder might expect dividends.

4   Include: fund replacement of old / purchase of extra equipment; move to a new factory; take over business.

Examination-style questions

a   Advantages: no interest to pay, no need to repay, better than keeping unneeded assets. Disadvantages: take time to sell, unknown value and may not have any to sell.

b   Points include: cost of finance, amount of retained profit, current level of debt, time, purpose, amount needed, risk involved, control.

c   Student's own answer based on points discussed. Issue shares – no need to repay so no increase to debt; no interest payable so expenses do not increase; risk of takeover if too many shares sold so the business loses control; less control for existing shareholders so they lose influence. Debt – opposite of advantages and disadvantages of equity, plus ability to raise sufficient funds.

d   Points could include: **Profit** – no need to repay, no interest or monthly outflows, own it, no money left for emergencies especially as profits fell to $1m last year. **Leasing** – not owned, can return when need, profit kept for emergency but negative impact on cash flow. **Issue shares** – see points in (c) plus private limited company - only sell to friends and family could limit amount. Conclusion based on points discussed.

Application for questions b–d could include: private limited company, $5m, profits fell, $1m, new technology, no non-current assets to sell.

Unit 20

Progress check

1   Points include: to pay employees, suppliers or other trade payables.

2   It shows timings of money flowing into and out of a business over a period of time.

3   Options include: rent, wages, raw materials, insurance, advertising.

4   Working capital = current assets – current liabilities. Cash is only one part of working capital.

Examination-style questions

a   The amount of cash left at the end of the period.

b   Closing balance (X) $70; net cash flow (Y) $40.

c   There is competition so cash inflow is reduced; amount of wasted fruit and veg / high cost of supplies produces higher outflows; sales and inventory costs fluctuate each month so it is difficult to plan.

d   Options include: arrange overdraft – access to cash when needed to pay trade payables reduce costs to lower outflows; delay payments to trade payables so there is more time for inflows from sales; ask trade receivables to pay quicker so cash inflows are received sooner; factoring; sell surplus fixed assets; sell inventory cheaply so receive cash quickly;

Application for questions c–d could include: appropriate use of numbers, market stall, fruit and vegetables, supermarket, low prices and more products.

Unit 21

Progress check

1   Profit is what is left over from revenue after all costs have been paid.

2   The income and expenditure of business over a given period of time.

3   Wages (if linked to actual production) and inventory costs.

4   Expenses.

Examination-style questions

a   The income of business from sale of products sold in a period of time.

b   Gross profit (X) = $12m; Retained profit (Y) = $4m.

c   Lack of finance – lenders unwilling to lend as the business is seen as higher risk; damaged reputation could affect sales; negative impact on employees' motivation so they become less productive.

d   Options include ways to lower costs (for example, cost of sales or expenses) or increase revenue (widen market or range of products, increase prices).

Application for questions c–d could include: appropriate use of numbers, books, competitive market, website, fall in profit, expansion, 60 shops.

Unit 22

Progress check

1   Debts which have to be paid back in less than one year, such as overdraft, trade payables.

2   Land, machinery and buildings.

3   Net assets.

4   A particular point in time.

Examination-style questions

a   Short-term assets which will last less than a year.

b   Bank overdraft, trade payables.

c   Non-current assets increased – more machinery; current assets increased – more inventory; shareholder equity – more capital or profit made.

d   Lenders – level of finance; shareholders – return on their investment; government – size of business; employees – worth of business.

Application for questions c–d could include: appropriate use of numbers, forks and spoons, increased demand, increase production.

Unit 23

Progress check

1   It helps to judge business performance.

2   Current and acid test ratios.

3    $\dfrac{\text{Profit}}{\text{Capital}} \times 100$

4   Include employees, lenders, shareholders, government, community, suppliers.

Examination-style questions

a   (144 / 720) × 100 = 20%

b   Impossible to predict future; need to compare against other businesses; other business might not have used the same way to measure values; other factors affect performance.

c   Trade payables – can pay for inventory; employees – pay or security; lenders – repay loans; investors – possible returns on investment.

d   Gross profit margin (32% to 33.3%) – improved so prices increased more than cost of sales or cost of sales lower. Profit margin improved (15% to 20%) – better control of expenses; ROCE fallen slightly – so less successful in generating profit from capital. There is mixed news for the Finance Director.

Application for questions c–d could include: appropriate use of numbers, bicycles, recession, invest in new machinery.

Unit 24

Progress check

1 It is a general rise in the level of prices over time.

2 Economic growth, low unemployment, positive balance of payments, low inflation.

3 Economic growth, boom, recession, slump

4 Finance costs will increase.

Examination-style questions

a It is a period in the business cycle when economic growth is rising rapidly.

b Options include: government spending, interest rates, legal controls, tariffs.

c Consumers will have less disposal income so will reduce spending; there will be less retained profit, which reduces this source of internal finance; prices will be higher which can lower demand for luxury products.

d Higher labour costs increase expenses; increased competition can lower demand; risk of inflation pushes up costs and prices.

Application for questions c–d could include: economic boom, employment is high, new businesses, electrical products, 200 skilled employees, high profits.

Unit 25

Progress check

1 Pollution, loss of space, use up resources, waste, global warming.

2 External benefits and external costs.

3 Development which meets the needs of the present population without damaging the ability of future generations to meet their own needs.

4 Legal means rules that cannot be ignored. A business does not have to be ethical.

Examination-style questions

a A group of people who come together with a common aim to try to influence the activities and decisions of businesses or government.

b Jobs created, forms of pollution, waste, risk of global warming.

c A boycott, which will lower sales; lobby government/business to raise awareness of issues; petitions or demonstrations to create publicity.

Application for questions b–c could include: recycled waste plastic, deliveries, old factory, 30 more employees, 1000 or 25 000 blocks, new site.

Unit 26

Progress check

1 Tariffs affect prices while a quota affects the quantity of imports.

2 To access larger markets, spread risk, access new materials, have lower costs or access to better/different skills, be closer to market.

3 No. A multinational business must have operations such as factories in other countries.

4 Currency depreciation helps exporters.

Examination-style questions

a It means that import taxes are put on the price of goods entering the country.

b Larger target market increases sales and lowers costs (for example, transport, distribution, labour and material costs) so profits can increase; possible help from government which can lower costs; avoid legal barriers so the business is able to produce more.

c **Appreciation**: imports are relatively cheaper – lower costs can increase profit for same sales. **Tariff**: increases cost so prices may have to rise, lowering demand.

d Points could include: **Jobs** – 400 new jobs - lower unemployment which is currently high - less money for govt to pay out/increased tax received - vmore spending in local economy so as long as other factors can be managed this could be seen as most important factor. **Pollution** – increased traffic leading to congestion so difficult / longer to move between places; however this could be issue whichever business opens up. **Competition** – leads to more choice/lower prices which could benefit consumers if goods sold locally, however local businesses may struggle to survive against MNC competitor - reducing choice. Conclusion based on points discussed.

Application for questions b–d could include: health care products, factory, large target market, lot of competition, tariffs, exchange rates, 400 employees, high unemployment.

Sample case studies

These exam-style case studies have been written by the author and are designed to provide you with additional practice material.

Case study 1

Fizzed Fruits (FF) is a successful private limited company. It produces a wide range of fruit drinks which are sold all over country J. FF plans to expand overseas to take advantage of the opportunities from globalisation. FF has invested a lot of money in new technology in order to meet the planned extra demand. All drinks are made using batch production. Motivation is poor and many employees leave.

FF has recently launched a new citrus drink called 'Full on Fruit'. It is targeted at the mass market where there are many unbranded drinks available. A high price has been set. It is sold in the popular FF cartons and advertised locally on radio and through in-store promotions. The drinks are sold directly to independent shops.

The Finance Director is disappointed with the initial sales of the new drink. He is concerned about its cash flow position. He said, 'What will this mean for working capital? Our suppliers are already complaining. Where is the market research?'

Appendix 1: Advertising poster for a rival product.

Don't settle for less — Drink the best
Wake it Up! Shake it Up!
Get Juiced up!
Rated the number one drink in Taste

Magazine awards for 2016

Available in Supermarkets Everywhere

Appendix 2: Memo to Finance Director

To: Finance Director
From: Production department
Subject: Estimated production costs for 'Full on Fruit'

Price per litre	$2
Variable costs per litre	$1.20
Fixed costs per week (including packaging)	$2000

Materials costs are high as we import most of the fruit. The distinctive cartons are also expensive, but these are part of the brand.

Appendix 3: News bulletin

News Everyday (31 December 2016)

Interest rates went up by 0.5% last month. Further increases are expected next year. Many businesses are worried about how this might affect them.

Questions

1 a Explain **two** benefits to FF of calculating break-even sales for the new drink.

Benefit 1:

Benefit 2: [8]

   b Consider the advantages and disadvantages of the following **three** ways FF could use to improve its cash flow position. Which way do you think FF should use? Justify your answer.

Overdraft:

Delaying payments to suppliers:

Ask customers to pay more quickly:

Recommendation: [12]

2 a Explain **one** advantage and **one** disadvantage to FF of using batch production.

Advantage:

Disadvantage: [8]

   b Explain why the following **three** factors are important to FF when deciding whether to introduce new technology. Which factor do you think is most important? Justify your answer.

Capital to invest:

Employee's reaction to change:

Ability to produce new products:

Conclusion: [12]

3 a Explain **two** ways in which FF could use market research information.

Way 1:

Way 2: [8]

   b Consider the advantages and disadvantages of the following **three** changes FF could make to its marketing mix. Which one of these changes do you think FF should choose? Justify your answer.

Lower price:

Sell product in large supermarkets:

Advertise on social media networks:

Conclusion: [12]

4 a Explain **two** ways in which an increase in interest rates might affect FF.

 Way 1:

 Way 2: [8]

 b Explain how the following **three** changes are likely to affect FF when importing its ingredients. Which one of these changes is likely to have the most effect on FF? Justify your answer.

 Appreciation of exchange rate in country J:

 Introduction of an import quota:

 Poor harvest in other countries:

 Conclusion: [12]

Case study 2

Solid Metal Mining (SMM) is a large multinational company. It has copper, nickel and other mines in ten countries. SMM's main objectives are growth and profit. Last year SMM's profits were $36m.

SMM uses hi-tech machinery and unskilled workers. All employees do a 12-hour shift and are paid the minimum wage in each country. Employees also receive a bonus based on each mine's profits. Some basic training is provided, but the health and safety record is poor and motivation is low.

Recently, large amounts of copper have been found in country L. Some people are worried about the damage that mining will cause local wildlife. Opening the new mine will be expensive for SMM as it will need $50m for the mining equipment. SMM will also have to build roads to the site. The new mine will create 500 new jobs.

There are many communication barriers affecting SMM.

Appendix 1: Extract from SMM's accounts.

Statement of financial position as at 31 December 2016 ($m)		
Non-current assets		320
Current assets	60	
Current liabilities	80	
Net assets		300
Financed by:		
Share capital	120	
Retained profit	100	
Non-current liabilities	80	
Capital employed		300

Appendix 2: Article in national newspaper

Mining row refuses to go away!

Protests continue about the decision to allow SMM to open a new mine. Environmental groups had hoped to obtain funding for an eco-tourism project at the country's main beauty spot.

A Government minister said, 'Unemployment is high. People need economic growth, not green spaces.'

Appendix 3: Map of proposed site.

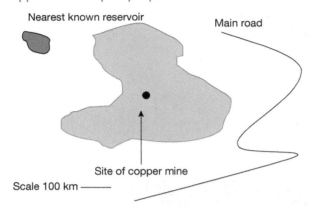

Nearest known reservoir

Main road

Site of copper mine

Scale 100 km ———

Questions

1 a Explain **two** measures SMM could take to improve its health and safety record.

Measure 1:

Measure 2: [8]

  b Consider the advantages and disadvantages of following **three** methods SMM could use to improve employee motivation. Which method do you think SMM should use? Justify your answer.

Profit sharing:

Job rotation:

Training:

Conclusion: [12]

2 a Explain **two** possible reasons why SMM wants to grow.

Reason 1:

Reason 2: [8]

  b State the advantages and disadvantages of the following **three** methods of communication SMM could use to communicate with its employees. Which method do you think SMM should use? Justify your answer.

Notice boards:

Meetings:

Text messages:

Recommendation: [12]

3 a Explain **two** possible reasons why profit might be important to SMM.

Reason 1:

Reason 2: [8]

b Consider the advantages and disadvantages of the following **three** sources of finance SMM could use. Which source of finance do you think SMM should use? Justify your answer.

Retained profits:

Share issue:

Bank loan:

Conclusion: [12]

4 a SMM will need to recruit employees for the mine. Explain **two** stages of the recruitment process SMM should use.

Stage 1:

Stage 2: [8]

b Explain how the following **three** stakeholder groups are likely to be affected by the opening of the new mine. Which stakeholder group do you think will be most affected? Justify your answer.

Local community:

Customers:

Government:

Conclusion: [12]

Mark schemes for the case studies

The mark schemes that appear here have been written by the author. The way marks are awarded in examination may be different.

Part a questions

Marks are awarded in this way:

Knowledge [k] (2×1) – award one mark for each relevant point.
Analysis [an] (2×1) – award one mark for a relevant explanation.
Application [ap] (2×2) – award two application marks for each point.

Part b questions

Level	Knowledge/Analysis/Evaluation
3	9–10 marks well-justified recommendation 7–8 marks for some limited judgement in recommendation
2	4–6 marks Detailed discussion of points
1	1–3 marks Outline possible issues – 1 mark per statement
0	Zero marks. No creditworthy response

Award up to 2 marks for relevant application (see 1a of relevant case study).

Level 1 – 1 mark for each L1 statement (maximum 3), for example identifies factor, method or issue.

Level 2 – one L2 explanation can gain 4 marks and a further mark for each additional L2 explanation (maximum 6).
Level 3 – there must be at least two L2 marks awarded, and a recommendation that justifies the decision made.

Case study 1

1 a Explain **two** benefits to FF of calculating break-even sales for the new drink. [8]

Knowledge (2x1) – award one mark for each relevant benefit.
Analysis (2x1) – award one mark for a relevant explanation.
Application (2x1) – award two application marks for each benefit.

Relevant benefits include:
- sales target to aim for
- it will show if the fixed costs are too high
- can see impact on break-even sales if price is changed.

For example: Have a sales target to aim for [k] so that the business will know if sales of cartons are not reaching its weekly target [ap]. The business can then do something such as more advertising to attract more customers [an].

Application marks may be awarded for appropriate use of the following:
- price similar to unbranded items, disappointing initial sales, suppliers' complaints, use of information in Appendix 2, imported fruit, packaging, lot of money on new technology, private limited company, successful, poor motivation, many leave.

1 b Consider the advantages and disadvantages of the following **three** ways FF could use to improve its cash flow position. Which way do you think FF should use? Justify your answer. [12]

Mark scheme:

Factor	Possible points might include:
Overdraft	• Flexible – so only use when needed – which can reduce amount of interest payable • Can be quick to arrange • Repayable on demand – which could increase cash flow problems rather than help resolve
Delaying payments to suppliers	• Reduce cash outflows – allowing more time to generate cash from the drinks • Suppliers could refuse to supply ingredients – stopping or delaying production
Ask customers to pay more quickly	• Would make cash available sooner • Customers may be unable or unwilling to pay sooner – leading to reduced demand – reducing cash inflows
Recommendation	• Suppliers are already complaining – further delaying payments could increase risk of suppliers refusing to provide ingredients • Customers are independent retailers – who may not be able to pay quicker – but may be able to change terms which could help both parties • Overdraft may be best choice – expensive to arrange – but will not damage relations with suppliers or customers

2 a Explain **one** advantage and **one** disadvantage to FF of using batch production. [8]

Relevant points might include

Advantages:
- flexible
- production can be easily changed from one product to another
- some variety of jobs.

Disadvantages:
- increased storage costs
- time delay while there is a switch between batches
- a fault in a part of the batch can affect the whole batch.

For example: Flexible [k] production can be easily changed from one drink to another [ap] so if the initial sales for the new drink do improve [ap], FF will be able to respond quickly to meet the increase in demand [an].

2 b Explain why the following **three** factors are important to FF when deciding whether to introduce new technology. Which factor do you think is most important? Justify your answer. [12]

Mark scheme:

Factor	Possible points might include:
Capital to invest	• Provides money to invest in new machines – no need to borrow money – no repayment • Opportunity cost – as funds not available for other purposes
Employee's reaction to change	• Employees may be resistant to change – lower motivation – could reduce productivity and output • Opportunity to learn new skills – so could allow them to gain promotion or extra pay • Training can be offered
Ability to produce new products	• Can help it remain / increase competitiveness – important as facing competition from rival manufacturer • Able to enter new markets – spread risk • May not guarantee sales if products are not fully researched / no demand
Conclusion	• New products – can help FF enter new markets – but no guarantee that new products will be successful – based on latest new product • If new technology helps employees, they may accept the changes especially if training provided and chance for promotion / increased pay • Capital to invest – may be most important, as it is needed to purchase the machinery – if business cannot afford it, then not able to produce new products and there are ways to address employees' concerns

3 a Explain **two** ways FF could use market research information. [8]

Relevant points might include:
- find out level of competition
- size of market

- help set prices
- know which methods of promotion to use
- find out best places to sell its products
- where are competitors' products are sold.

For example: Find out the level of competition [k]. If other juice makers have a large market share [ap], it will be difficult for FF to compete [an]. Brand loyalty to the other products will reduce the potential market for the new drink.

3 b Consider the advantages and disadvantages of the following **three** changes FF could make to its marketing mix. Which one of these changes do you think FF should choose? Justify your answer. [12]

Mark scheme:

Change	Possible points might include:
Lower price	• Could encourage more people to try it – as more affordable • Could damage image as may not be seen as a high quality product • May not cover the costs of production
Sell product in large supermarkets	• Able to compete directly against rival • Supermarkets buy in large quantities increasing sales opportunities • Supermarkets may demand discount reducing its profit margin
Advertise on social media networks	• Can attract new or different audience • Existing or new customers may not have access to network • Lower cost of advertising than radio – which could be important when cash flow is a concern • Easier to update
Conclusion	• Lower prices may affect image – risk to reputation could limit effectiveness of option – also reaction of rivals • Supermarkets can widen market – and allow it to compete directly against rival – but may not be able to have as much say over how it is promoted in store • Social media – can target audience – cheaper to do than current option – so may be better than the other options

4 a Explain **two** ways in which an increase in interest rates might affect FF. [8]

Relevant points might include:
- increased cost of new bank loan
- increased cost of overdraft
- higher mortgage costs for customers reduce spending
- lower sales as consumers reduce spending
- lower profits as costs higher
- higher interest rates attract more savings from customer or company.

For example: Increased cost of bank loan [k] will increase costs as the interest paid on the loan will be more than before [an]. This might reduce profit unless FF can increase the prices it charges for its drinks [ap]. As initial sales are low, and it has a lot of competition, this does not seem likely [ap].

4 b Explain how the following **three** changes are likely to affect FF when importing its ingredients. Which one of these changes is likely to have the most effect on FF? Justify your answer. [12]

Mark scheme:

Factor	Possible points might include:
Appreciation of exchange rates in country J	• Imports become cheaper – leading to lower costs for FF to buy its ingredients – so prices could be reduced – leading to increased sales helping FF to remain competitive
Introduction of an import quota	• Fixed quantity allowed to be imported – leading to shortage of fruit – so not able to produce as much or it could restrict which products they can produce – could lead to lower sales.
Poor harvest in other countries	• Reduced supply of fruit – leading to higher material costs – which could increase prices • May have to look for suppliers in different countries or change / remove some products
Conclusion	• Poor harvest will limit supply of fruit – depends on whether alternative supplies can be obtained – may have to pay more but may not stop production • If currency appreciates, this helps lower costs, and could help FF lower prices and gain sales but only if able to buy sufficient supplies • Quota will limit supply – and how much FF can produce as it imports its ingredients so whichever country they come from (unless own) the quota will have an impact – so depending on limit introduced, this could have most effect.

Case study 2

1 a Explain **two** measures that SMM could take to improve its health and safety record. [8]

Relevant points might include:
• additional training
• recruit skilled workers to operate machinery
• provide safety equipment
• improve working conditions, for example lights
• posters and safety leaflets
• reduce hours.

For example: Additional training [k] so that employees have a better understanding of what they need to do [an] when it comes to operating the high tech equipment [ap]. The basic training might not cover everything and mistakes could happen [ap].

Application marks may be awarded for appropriate use of the following:

• poor record, basic training, unskilled workers, 12-hour shift, high tech machinery, mines or related terms, for example nickel, copper, 500 jobs, growth, employment, use of numbers, eco-tourism, wildlife, environmental groups, green space.

1 b Consider the advantages and disadvantages of following **three** methods SMM could use to improve employee motivation. Which method do you think SMM should use? Justify your answer. [12]

Mark scheme:

Method	Possible points might include:
Profit sharing	• Incentive to work hard to gain share of business success • Increase cost to business • Other factors affect level of profit
Job rotation	• Makes the job more interesting • Lower labour turnover • May not be very easy for all employees to switch between different jobs – some tasks may not be carried out effectively
Training	• Improve skills – could help increase productivity • Cost of training – adds to expenses
Conclusion	• Profit share – other factors affect level of profit so hard work may not be rewarded • Job rotation – may not be easy to switch between tasks – increasing risk of accidents • Training – although adds to business costs – will ensure employees have necessary skills – especially as only basic training given – allowing them to introduce job enrichment later – so probably best choice

2 a Explain **two** possible reasons why SMM wants to grow. [8]

Relevant points might include:
• gain economies of scale, for example technical, purchasing
• greater recognition
• profitability
• spread risk
• more customers.

For example: Purchasing economies of scale [k] as SMM can buy equipment in large quantities [ap]. The business will then be able to lower average costs [an], which can help improve its profits [ap].

2 b State the advantages and disadvantages of the following **three** methods of communication SMM could use to communicate with its employees. Which method do you think SMM should use? Justify your answer. [12]

Mark scheme:

Method	Relevant points
Notice boards	• Can be placed in key locations • Easy to miss / torn down • Possible language problems
Meetings	• Allows for two way communication • Difficult / expensive to organise as employees work in different locations at different times

Method	Relevant points
Text messages	• Can be read when suits employees • Internet problems or poor signal • Employees may not have read message
Recommendation	• Notice boards – can be visual – useful for key messages but can be easily damaged • Meetings – allow for two way communication which is important – but cost and difficulty of getting everyone together when they work 12-hour shifts • Text messages – limited information, no way of knowing if message gets through – but can read when suits persons – option for feedback – so probably best choice

3 a Explain **two** possible reasons why profit might be important to SMM. [8]

Relevant points might include:
• reward for risk-taking
• measure of success
• source of internal finance
• needed for long-term survival.

For example: Reward for risk-taking [k]. SMM owners will have put their money at risk, as there is no guarantee that enough copper or minerals will be found [ap]. If the mine is not successful, they will lose the money invested [ap], so they want some reward for this risk [an].

3 b Consider the advantages and disadvantages of the following **three** sources of finance SMM could use. Which source of finance do you think SMM should use? Justify your answer. [12]

Mark scheme:

Method	Relevant points
Retained profits	• No need to repay which means no additional expenses • Opportunity cost – as funds used are not available for other purposes or in an emergency • Have sufficient profits - as $100m - so $50m left
Share issue	• No need to repay • Shareholders may expect larger dividend • Risk of loss of control
Bank loan	• Need to repay which increases expenses • Obtain full amount • Time to repay – could be able to generate income to make repayments
Conclusion	• Share issue – no need to repay, but increased risk of loss of control • Bank loan will provide a long term option – but cost of repayment must be considered • Do SMM have the capital to invest – if so, retained profits probably the best option

4　a　SMM will need to recruit employees for the mine. Explain **two** stages of the recruitment process SMM should use.　　　　[8]

Relevant points might include:
- job analysis
- job description
- person specification
- job advertisement
- interviews.

For example: The job description will list all the tasks that need to be done [k], such as digging for copper [ap]. This will make it easier for SMM to select appropriate mine workers. [ap], as they will not receive applications from people not prepared to do the work [an].

4　b　Explain how the following **three** stakeholder groups are likely to be affected by the opening of the new mine. Which stakeholder group do you think will be most affected? Justify your answer.　　　　[12]

Mark scheme:

Method	Relevant points
Local community	• Damage to environment – which could impact on health due to noise and air pollution • Jobs created – money into local economy • Loss of eco-tourism • Remote location – could improve infrastructure allowing other business opportunities • Mines can be dangerous – risk of accidents
Customers	• Increased supply of local copper – so less need to import from other countries – reducing costs of import and time to receive • Quality of copper may not be suitable for purposes so do not benefit
Government	• Lower unemployment – from new jobs created – improving standards of living and reduce unemployment payments • Increase in locally sourced materials • Tax receipts – to be able to provide services but will the MNC expect incentives or pay full amount of tax? • Environmental damage
Conclusion	• Customers – benefit from not having to import copper but MNC may set high prices so limited benefit • Government – gain from lower unemployment and tax payments – but may face protests especially from environmental groups – may lose power – but used to having to face difficult decisions • Local community – may benefit from jobs, but are directly affected by environmental concerns – probably most affected.

Index